BERTOLT BRECHT

The Caucasian Chalk Circle

Translated from the German by
JAMES *and* TANIA STERN
with W.H. AUDEN

With Commentary and Notes by
HUGH RORRISON

Methuen Student Editions
METHUEN DRAMA

Methuen Student Edition

First published in 1984 by Methuen London Ltd by arrangement with
Suhrkamp Verlag, Frankfurt am Main.
Reissued with a new cover 1994

17 19 20 18 16

Methuen Publishing Limited
215 Vauxhall Bridge Road, London SW1V 1EJ

Peribo Pty Ltd, 58 Beaumont Road, Mount Kuring-Gai
NSW 2080, Australia, ACN 002 273 761 (for Australia and New Zealand)

Methuen Publishing Limited Reg. No. 3543167

Printed and bound in Great Britain
by Cox & Wyman Ltd, Reading, Berkshire

ISBN 0 413 54450 8

Papers used by Methuen Publishing Limited
are natural, recyclable products made from wood grown in
sustainable forests. The manufacturing processes conform to
the environmental regulations of the country of origin

*Thanks are due to John Willet, and to Herta Ramthun of the
Brecht Archive, for help in the preparation of this edition.*

Contents

Azdak (Ernst Busch) on the Judge's seat with Shauva (Harry Gillmann) in attendance. From the Berliner Ensemble production. (Photo: Percy Paukschta).

Bertolt Brecht 1898–1956

Brecht's life falls into three distinct phases demarcated by his forced exile from his native Germany during the Hitler years. From 1898-1933 he is in Germany; from 1933-1947 he is in exile in various parts of the world; in 1947 he returns to Europe, first to Switzerland then to Berlin.

Germany

1898   Eugen Berthold Friedrich Brecht born on 10 February at Augsburg where his father was an employee and later director of the Haindl paper mill.

1908   Brecht goes to Augsburg Grammar School (Realgymnasium) where he is an indifferent pupil and a rebel in his quiet way, numbering among his friends Caspar Neher, later his designer. Brecht was almost expelled for taking a dismissive, anti-patriotic line when set an essay with the title 'It is a sweet and honourable thing to die for one's country'.

1917   Brecht enrols as a medical student at Munich University, where he also attends Arthur Kutscher's theatre seminar. He samples the bohemian literary life of the city.

1918   Brecht is conscripted and serves as a medical orderly, though he still lives at home. He writes *Baal*, a rumbustious, even outrageous dramatic tribute to natural drives and anarchic sexuality, and does theatre reviews for the local newspaper, *Augsburger Neueste Nachrichten*.

1919   Brecht writes *Drums in the Night*. He meets the comedian Karl Valentin, the theatre director Erich Engel, and actresses Elisabeth Bergner, Blandine Ebinger, Carola Neher and Marianne Zoff.

1920   Brecht visits Berlin.

1921   Brecht's registration at Munich University is cancelled. An attempt to make himself known in literary circles in Berlin ends with him in hospital suffering from malnutrition. His new friendship with Arnolt Bronnen, the playwright, leads him to change the spelling of his name to Bertolt, or Bert.

1922   Brecht marries Marianne Zoff. He writes *In the Jungle of Cities*.

1923 Brecht's daughter Hanne is born. The activities of Hitler's
National Socialists are hotly discussed in Brecht's Munich
circle. The first productions of *In the Jungle of Cities* and
Baal take place in Munich and Leipzig respectively.

1924 Brecht directs Christopher Marlowe's *Edward II* which he
and Lion Feuchtwanger had adapted. He was already using
certain devices (plot summaries before scenes, white face
make-up to indicate fear) to induce critical detachment in
actors and audience. He finally settles in Berlin and is taken
on as dramaturg (literary adviser) at Max Reinhardt's
Deutsches Theater. The actress Helen Weigel bears him a
son, Stefan.

1925 Klabund's *The Chalk Circle,* premiered at Frankfurt and
Hanover in January, is directed in Berlin in October by Max
Reinhardt with Elisabeth Bergner in the female lead.

1926 *Man Equals Man* premiered at Darmstadt and Düsseldorf.
The Elephant Calf, an accompanying 'interlude for the
foyer', parodies the *Chalk Circle* test. Brecht's work on a play
(which he never finished) called *Joe Fleischhacker,* which
was to deal with the Chicago Wheat Exchange, leads him to
the study of Marx as the only adequate method of
analysing the workings of capitalism.

1927 Brecht divorces Marianne Zoff. He works with Erwin
Piscator, the pioneer of communist political theatre in
Germany, on a dramatisation of Hasek's novel *The Good
Soldier Schweik.*

1928 *The Threepenny Opera,* music by Kurt Weill, words by
Brecht (based on a translation of John Gay's *Beggar's Opera*
by Brecht's friend and collaborator Elisabeth Hauptmann)
opens at the Theater am Schiffbauerdamm and becomes the
hit of the season. Brecht had provocatively transferred
bourgeois manners to a Soho criminal setting.

1929 Brecht marries Helene Weigel. *The Baden-Baden Cantata* is
staged at the Baden-Baden Music Festival, music by
Hindemith.

1930 Brecht's daughter Barbara born. His *Lehrstück* or didactic
play, *The Measures Taken,* is given its first performance in
Berlin. The communist didactic plays for amateur
performance were intended to clarify the ideas of the
performers as much as the audience. The first performance
of *The Rise and Fall of the City of Mahogonny,* an opera
with words by Brecht and music by Kurt Weill causes a riot

as the Nazis voice their criticism at Leipzig. In his notes on
the opera Brecht tabulates the differences between the
traditional *dramatic* (or Aristolelian) and the new *epic* (or
non-Aristolelian) theatre at which he is aiming.

1931   Brecht completes *St Joan of the Stockyards*.

1932   Brecht's only film, *Kuhle Wampe*, is held up by the censor.
        His dramatisation of Maxim Gorky's novel *The Mother* is
        performed by a left-wing collective in Berlin, music by Hanns
        Eisler. It demonstrates the development of a worker's
        mother towards proletarian class-consciousness. Beginning
        of Brecht's friendship with Margarete Steffin. Brecht studies
        Marxism under the dissident communist Karl Korsch.

Exile

1933   The Nazis come to power. The night after the German
        parliament building (the Reichstag) is burnt down, Brecht
        flees with his family to Prague. He moves to Vienna, then
        Zurich, finally settling on the island of Fyn in Denmark.
        His friendship with Ruth Berlau begins.

1934   Brecht visits London. The themes of flight and exile enter
        his poetry.

1935   Brecht is stripped of his German citizenship. He visits
        Moscow and meets the Soviet dramatist Sergei Tretiakov.
        He attends the International Writers' Conference in Paris.
        He visits New York to look in on a production of *The
        Mother*, which does not meet with his approval.

1936   Brecht attends the International Writers' Conference in
        London. He writes anti-fascist poetry.

1937   Brecht attends the International Writers' Conference in
        Paris.

1938   Brecht finishes writing *Life of Galileo*. *Fear and Misery of
        The Third Reich* is given its first performance in Paris.
        Brecht makes notes for an 'Odense' *Chalk Circle* which was
        to be set in Denmark in the 11th century.

1939   Brecht moves to Stockholm with his family. He finishes
        writing *Mother Courage and Her Children*.

1940   German forces march into Denmark. In Lidingö Brecht
        completes *The Augsburg Chalk Circle*, a short story set
        in the Thirty Years War. Brecht's household moves to
        Helsinki in Finland where his friendship with the writer
        Hella Wuolijoki begins.

1941   Brecht completes *Mr Puntila and his Man Matti*, *The Good

Person of Szechwan and *The Resistable Rise of Arturo Ui*.
He writes war poetry and 'Finnish Epigrams'. Leaving
Finland Brecht travels through the Soviet Union via
Leningrad and Moscow (where Margarete Steffin dies) to
Vladivostock and sails to the U.S.A. He arrives in Los
Angeles in July and settles with his family in Santa Monica.
He makes contact with other exiles (Heinrich Mann,
Lion Feuchtwanger and Fritz Lang, the film director) and
with the natives (Orson Welles). First performance of
Mother Courage and Her Children in neutral Switzerland.

1942   Brecht prepares his *Poems in Exile* for publication. He
participates in the anti-war, anti-fascist activities of exile
groups. He meets Charles Laughton.

1943   The first performances of *The Good Person of Szechwan*
and of *Life of Galileo* take place in Zurich.

1944   Brecht becomes a member of the newly formed Council
for a Democratic Germany. The Red Army drives the
Germans out of the Caucasus. Following a Broadway
contract for the play, arranged by the actress Luise Rainer,
Brecht writes the first version of *The Caucasian Chalk
Circle*, and almost immediately starts reworking it. W.H.
Auden works on an English version with his friends James
and Tania Stern. Brecht studies Arthur Waley's translations
of Chinese poetry.

1945   *Fear and Misery of the Third Reich* is given its first English
performance in New York under the title *The Private Life
of the Master Race*. Brecht and Charles Laughton complete
an English version of *Life of Galileo*.

1946   The first performance of Brecht's adaptation of Webster's
The Duchess of Malfi takes place in Boston.

1947   Charles Laughton appears in the title role of *Life of Galileo*
in Beverly Hills and New York. Brecht appears before the
House Committee on Unamerican Activities and proves
himself a master of ambiguity when cross-examined about
his communist sympathies.

Return

Brecht and Helene Weigel go to Zurich, leaving their son
Stefan, who is an American citizen, in the U.S.A. He meets
Max Frisch, his old friend and designer Caspar Neher, and
the playwright Carl Zuckmayer.

1948   Brecht's adaptation of *Antigone of Sophocles* is performed in Chur, Switzerland, and *Mr Puntila and his Man Matti* is given its first performance in Zurich. He publishes the *Little Organum for the Theatre*. Brecht travels to Berlin and starts rehearsals of *Mother Courage* at the Deutsches Theater in the Soviet sector of the city. *The Caucasian Chalk Circle* is first performed in Eric and Maja Bentley's English translation by students at Northfield, Minnesota.

1949   *Mother Courage* opens at the Deutsches Theater with Helene Weigel in the title role. Brecht visits Zurich again before settling in Berlin. The *Berliner Ensemble*, Brecht and Helene Weigel's own state-subsidised company, is formed and opens with *Puntila*. The second version of *The Caucasian Chalk Circle* is published in East Berlin by the literary magazine *Sinn und Form*. Brecht applies for an Austrian passport (H. Weigel is Austrian).

1951   *The Mother* is performed by the *Berliner Ensemble*. Brecht finishes the first version of his adaptation of Shakespeare's *Coriolanus*.

1953   Brecht is elected President of this German section of the PEN Club, the international writers' association. On 17 June there are strikes and demonstrations protesting about working conditions in the German Democratic Republic. Brecht writes a letter to the Secretary of the Socialist Unity Party which is released to the press in a doctored form.

1954   The Berliner Ensemble moves into its own home, the Theater am Schiffbauerdamm (where he had triumphed with *The Threepenny Opera* in 1928), and performs *The Caucasian Chalk Circle*. The prologue, *The Struggle for the Valley*, is now designated as Act I. Brecht makes public his objections to the Paris Treaty (which incorporated the Federal Republic of Germany into Nato) and to re-armament in general. The Berliner Ensemble's productions of *Mother Courage* and Kleist's *The Broken Pitcher* are enthusiastically received as the highlights of the Paris Théâtre des Nations festival. *Mother Courage* is awarded the prizes for best play and best production.

1955   Harry Buckwitz, directing the West German premiere of *The Caucasian Chalk Circle* at Frankfurt, omits *The Struggle for the Valley* as politically inopportune.

1956   Brecht is preparing the Berliner Ensemble, which by that time has become generally recognised as the foremost

progressive theatre in Europe, for a visit to London when
he dies of a heart attack on 14 August. The visit went ahead
and *Mother Courage*, *The Caucasian Chalk Circle*, and
Trumpets and Drums were presented at the Palace Theatre
at the end of August for a short season — a landmark in
Brecht's reception in the United Kingdom.

Pieter Brueghel's *Dulle Griet* (copyright A.C.L. Brussels)

Plot

As life returns to normal in the Soviet Caucasus after World War II an evacuated goat-breeding collective amicably agrees to forego its claim to its old valley so that a neighbouring collective fruit farm's irrigation scheme can go ahead. The two groups celebrate their accord with a performance of an ancient Chinese play, *The Chalk Circle*, under the guidance of a folk-singer.

The first part of the play shows how Grusha, a servant girl, gets engaged to Simon, a soldier, and then rescues the executed Governor's son during a palace revolution and flees with him to the northern mountains. After many perils she ends up marrying a sham invalid to provide for the child.

The second part tells the story of Azdak who goes to town to confess to a crime and is placed, by a quirk of fate, in the Judge's chair. His astutely biased judgements bring unwonted justice to the poor and needy, and when the Governor's widow brings an action against Grusha for the return of her son, he uses the chalk circle test to determine the true mother.

Scene 1: The Struggle for the Valley

Workers from two collective farms meet in a ruined village in the Caucasus after World War II under the chairmanship of an expert from the State Commission for Reconstruction. After a peasant and a young woman tractor driver have reflected on their part in the local guerilla campaign against the Germans, the Expert outlines the agenda. The evacuated 'Galinsk' collective wants to move its goats back into the valley, but the neighbouring 'Rosa Luxemburg' fruit farm has applied for the use of its former grazing lands. The two groups must themselves decide which of their projects should have priority.

After a brief protest about the limited time for discussion, an old goatherd hands round a sample of goat cheese. When a fruit farmer pronounces it excellent, the goatherd replies that it is nothing like the cheese they used to make on their own grassland. This causes some amusement, but the Expert takes his point; home is indeed where the bread tastes better, and your step is lighter.

A Soldier challenges the validity of legal rights and ancient possession, and a Girl Tractor Driver asserts that the law must constantly be scrutinized and brought up to date; but a Peasant Woman still objects to the state's confiscation of property, even if it does replace it. People are attached to their old hats, she says. Hats are one thing, land is quite another, says the Girl Tractor Driver.

The Expert now mediates. Land indeed has to be viewed as a tool, but a man's attachment to his native soil must be recognized. He invites the fruit farmers' Agronomist to present her project. She explains that a dam in the hills could make 300 hectares of barren land cultivable, but the project would only be viable if the 'Galinsk' valley could be incorporated.

When the goatherds counter with their new project for a stud farm, the Girl Tractor Driver recalls that they thought up their irrigation scheme when they were partisans in the hills; this allusion to the joint war effort serves to remind them of their hopes for a better future. The Girl Tractor Driver reflects that the home of the Soviet people should be the home of reason. When the plans for the irrigation scheme are unrolled they meet little opposition from the goatherds.

A play in honour of the 'Galinsk' delegation is announced to celebrate the agreement. It is to be performed by the fruit farmers under the direction of the famous folk-singer Arkady Cheidze. He explains that it is an old Chinese play called *The Chalk Circle* and will be done in traditional masks. It will take several hours and cannot be shortened, even though the Expert pleads he is in a hurry to get back to the capital.

Scene 2: The Noble Child

The Singer sings of Nukha, city of the damned in ancient times, when the Governor enjoyed life and the poor languished in misery; then Georgi Abashvili, the Governor, is shepherded through a crowd of beggars and petitioners by soldiers who dispense alms. His wife Natella Abashvili and the Fat Prince Kazbeki exchange hypocritical small talk in his wake. The Governor's baby coughs, starting a heated argument between his two rival doctors. A despatch rider tries unsuccessfully to deliver his message from the Persian war. The Singer conjures up the meeting at the city gate of Grusha Vachnadze, a palace maid, and Simon Chachava, a soldier. Grusha treats the amorous soldier, who has watched her hitching up her skirts to wash clothes in the river, with naive directness. The Singer

switches attention to the palace, now a trap full of armed men. The
Governor has noticed a suspicious discrepancy in the Fat Prince's
conversation but defers investigating it. He still refuses to hear the
despatch rider's message. As he leaves, his architects express
surprise that he is thinking of building with the war going so badly.
Screams are heard from the palace, the Governor is brought out in
chains, and his doctors and servants make themselves scarce. In the
confusion Simon comes looking for Grusha. He is to escort the
Governor's wife on her flight; Grusha calls him stubborn for
accepting this dangerous duty. Simon starts to propose and Grusha
interrupts to accept. She promises to wait two or three weeks until
the war is over. Nothing will have changed when he comes back. As
he leaves, the Governor's wife enters with the Adjutant,
complaining of migraine and snapping at the servants as she
moodily selects her travelling wardrobe, despite warnings that her
life is in danger. Only when the east gate goes up in flames does she
flee in horror, forgetting her child. A Stableman reports that the
Governor has been beheaded and that anyone found with the child
can expect no mercy. It is Grusha's turn to be stubborn as the
Cook tells her that gullible fools like herself always end up holding
the baby. Grusha puts the child down and goes to fetch her things.
By the time she comes back the Fat Prince who led the coup has
mounted the Governor's head over the gate and offered a reward
for the child. Grusha returns, hesitates and picks up the child, and
the Singer explains what is going through her mind as she watches
over it through the night and goes off towards morning carrying it.

Scene 3: The Flight into the Northern Mountains

The Singer announces Grusha's journey, the Musicians wonder
what fate awaits her and Grusha starts walking to the northern
mountains. To keep her spirits up she sings a folk-song about
incompetent generals. At a peasant's cottage an old man
overcharges her for milk for the baby. She tries to pass herself off
as a rich lady at a caravansary, but her worker's fingers give her
away and she is thrown out. A class-conscious servant offers to find
her some food, but she goes on her way. The Singer tells us she
wanders northwards, the Musicians wonder if she can elude the
pursuing Ironshirts. Two Ironshirts trudge on singing a ballad; the
sadistic Corporal tells his junior he is not a real soldier because he
does not enjoy violence. The Singer tells us the child is getting too
heavy for Grusha, the Musicians add that any habitation is
dangerous now. Grusha deposits Michael on a peasant's doorstep,

and the peasant woman decides to keep him despite her husband's protests. The Singer and the Musicians tell what Grusha is thinking as she walks away, only to encounter the two Ironshirts who question her menacingly. She turns and runs. Back at the cottage she pleads with the wife to take off the child's fine linen and pretend he is her own. In spite of Grusha's appeals to the woman's maternal feelings, she denies all knowledge of the child and the Corporal sends her outside in the custody of his man. As he examines the crib Grusha stuns him with a log and escapes with the baby. She stops at a stream and changes him into rags. In a poetic soliloquy she confesses that she has cared for the child too long to be able to part with him. Finally Grusha reaches a dangerous rope bridge over a ravine. Despite being told the bridge will break, Grusha crosses having told the child they must now live together or die together. From the other side she laughs at the Ironshirts. She comforts the child in the cold with a lullaby for the disinherited.

Scene 4: In the Northern Mountains
The Singer tells us that Grusha walks for seven days in the hope of a welcome from her brother Lavrenti. But he turns out to be hen-pecked, and his wife pious and heartless. Here the riots in the capital are just a distant rumour. The sister-in-law is more concerned about the cakes in the oven than the exhausted Grusha's condition. Grusha has to lie about having a husband. The winter passes. Grusha sings a ballad which expounds a strategy for survival: curl up small and hide in the middle of the crowd. Lavrenti tells her that people are talking about her fatherless child and she must leave in spring. The drip of melting snow is heard and Lavrenti makes a proposition. If Grusha will marry the dying peasant Yussup to legitimise Michael, Lavrenti will raid his wife's milk money and put up the dowry. In agreeing, Grusha is suddenly aware of the consequences of picking up the Governor's child back in Nukha. A comic wedding follows with a money-grabbing mother-in-law, a drunken monk, a bridegroom at death's door and a gossiping, gorging bunch of mourners-cum-wedding-guests. The sick bride-groom suddenly revives when there is talk that the war is over and the Grand Duke on the way back. Grusha faints, but Yussup gets out of bed and sends the guests packing. Now, the Singer observes, Grusha realises she has a husband. We see her scrubbing Yussup's back and listening to his abuse because she refuses to sleep with him. The Singer tells of time passing and

Michael growing. Michael plays at princes and governors with the other children and insists on his turn as the prince who chops off the governor's head. Simon Chachava appears in a ragged uniform and converses with Grusha from the far bank of the river. Grusha tells him cryptically that nothing has changed, but she has changed her name. The Singer fills in what she thought but did not say, namely that she had not the heart to leave a helpless child. As Simon turns to go he sees two Ironshirts taking away the child. They have orders to bring him back to the city. The Singer now observes that everything depends on the judge who tries the case of Natella Abashvili versus Grusha Vachnadze.

Scene 5: The Story of the Judge
The Singer goes back to the day the Grand Duke was overthrown and Governor Abashvili executed. On that day Azdak, a village clerk and a notorious drinker and poacher, shelters a fugitive in his hut. From his soft hands he identifies him as a member of the ruling classes; the man tries to bribe him, but Azdak still cannot bring himself to hand him over to the policeman Shauva when he comes to arrest Azdak on a poaching charge. Azdak talks Shauva into leaving empty-handed and then demonstrates to the man how poor people eat. By the next scene Azdak has realised that the man was the deposed Grand Duke, and he forces Shauva to take him under arrest to Nukha to confess his crime to the new regime, which he supposes to be revolutionary. They come upon some Ironshirts lounging at the foot of a gibbet on which the former Judge is swinging, and in a song Azdak reveals his sympathy for the revolution. There is a pause and an Ironshirt observes that there has just been a rising against the new rulers in the weavers' quarter which the Ironshirts put down for two piastres per weaver's head. Azdak realises he has misunderstood the situation and now reminds them that he actually let the Grand Duke get away. As he frenziedly denies all he said before, they drag him to the gallows — only to release him and guffaw at their hoax.

The Fat Prince who is the new ruler appears and proposes his nephew Bizergan Kazbeki to the Ironshirts for Judge. The Ironshirts as representatives of the people are to elect him, and they see this as a sign that, with the Grand Duke still unaccounted for, the Fat Prince feels insecure, so they can have some fun at his expense. Azdak is consulted and suggests a mock trial to put the nephew through his paces. He also suggests that they should try the Grand Duke, and volunteers to take his part. In the dock he claims that the war was declared on the advice of people like the Fat Prince and conducted by princes who kept out of the firing line and made vast profits in munitions and stores. The Fat Prince calls for his execution for these revolutionary views, but to his and Azdak's astonishment the Ironshirts, who have been amused by the performance and recognise the home truths it contained, proclaim Azdak Judge.

The Singer tells us that Azdak remained Judge during two years of civil war. Azdak judges two cases simultaneously, first inviting contributions and receives a bribe from the blackmailer. An Invalid accuses a Doctor (whose studies he had financed) of treating a patient free of charge and giving his benefactor an apoplectic stroke. The Doctor protests that he thought his servant had collected the fee, and the 'free' patient reports that the Doctor operated on the wrong leg anyway. Turning to the blackmail case, Azdak learns that the accused, when he chanced to enquire whether a landowner had really raped his own niece, had been assured that this was not the case and given money to enable his uncle to study music. Azdak considers the case proved, fines the blackmailer half his take to keep the landowner's name out of the case and suggests he study medicine for which he has an obvious talent. Then the Invalid is awarded free treatment, including any necessary amputation, in the event of another stroke. The Doctor is acquitted of an inexcusable professional error. The Singer comments that with justice blind and the truth obscure it takes a detached third party to right society's wrongs. Moving on, Azdak tries two further cases at a caravansary. An Innkeeper brings a case of rape on behalf of his son against a Stableman he found in the hay with his daughter-in-law Ludovica. After Azdak has seen Ludovica walk over and pick up a knife, he pronounces her guilty of assault with a deadly weapon, her bottom, and fines the Innkeeper the roan horse that he, Azdak, wants for himself. The Singer and the Musicians sing that Azdak has allayed the lower orders' fear of the law. In a tavern Azdak hears the case of the Old Woman versus the Farmers. She is in possession of a cow and some ham, allegedly provided miraculously by St. Banditus, but actually stolen from the Farmers by her brother-in-law, the Bandit Irakli, who appears in court in the guise of a wandering hermit, carrying a big axe. Azdak finds that for an old lady who has lost her son in the war to receive a ham is indeed a miracle and fines the Farmers for not believing in miracles. Again the Singer and the Musicians underline Azdak's role, which is to subvert the law in order to bring justice to the poor and needy. When the Singer announces the return of the Grand Duke, Azdak releases Shauva from his service, telling him he will soon be able to lick the hands of proper superiors again, for the days of disorder are over, but the new era has not yet come. Together they sing the Song of Chaos, which predicts the overthrow of the ruling classes. Azdak observes that the restoration of the Grand Duke means that the chance for change has been lost. He consults the book of statutes he has always sat on in court and pronounces that they will hang him for drunkenness because he helped poverty to its feet. Trembling with fear he decides to beg for mercy. When Natella Abashvili enters, he abjectly promises to have her son returned and Grusha beheaded. She sweeps off and Azdak follows her, bowing and scraping. Power has reverted to the old ruling class.

Scene 6: The Chalk Circle
Ironshirts lead Michael into court at Nukha. Grusha follows with the former Governor's Cook, who explains that Azdak is not a real judge, and if he is drunk she stands a chance. Grusha's story will be that Michael is her child, whom the Cook fostered. Simon Chachava, partly reconciled with Grusha, will claim he is the father. As the Ironshirts go off to search for the missing Azdak, Grusha and the Corporal she clubbed in the peasant's hut recognize one another. He makes no move, not wishing to reveal that he onced hunted for the child for the rival party. Natella Abashvili enters with her lawyers, who are trying to keep her calm. Azdak is brought on in chains and knocked about until he collapses. Defiant under the gallows, he is calling the Ironshirts bootlickers like himself when a despatch rider miraculously arrives with papers which, again, appoint Azdak as judge as a reward for sheltering the Grand Duke when he was on the run. The farmers who had denounced him are summarily marched off and Azdak, once he has recovered from the shock, reassumes the Judge's robes, takes his seat on the statute book and invites contributions. Relieved at this sign of 'normality' the Abashvili lawyers press bribes into his hand. Azdak asks what their fee is, saying he listens quite differently if he knows the advocates are good. He interrupts the lawyer's elaborate speech on bonds of blood and the holy ecstasies of love to hear what Grusha has to say, which is merely that the child is hers. When pressed, she asserts that she has brought him up as best she knew, has fed him, has spared no expense, and has taught him to work. The First Lawyer notes that she claims no blood bond. The

Second Lawyer expostulates that without Michael, Natella cannot get her hands on her estate or pay her lawyers. After the rival accounts of Michael's life, Azdak provocatively examines the strange affair of the woman who loves one man who claims to be the father of her child, is married to another, and yet takes offence at the suggestion that the child was conceived whoring. When Azdak decides to cut the proceedings short, Grusha accuses him of corruption and ignorance of the law, and calls him a lackey of the ruling classes. Azdak amusedly calls her to order and then, tiring of the case, turns to an old couple who, after forty years of marriage, want a divorce simply because they have never liked each other. He turns back to Grusha and asks if she would not prefer Michael to be rich. She says nothing, but thinks, as the Singer explains, that power and wealth corrupt. Azdak decides to put the case to the tug-of-war test. The child will be placed in a chalk circle, and the woman to pull him out will be the mother. The Lawyer protests on the grounds of his client's inferior strength, but Natella Abashvili wins the test twice. After the second attempt Grusha protests that she cannot tear apart a child she has reared. This is Azdak's cue to pronounce Grusha the true mother and advise her to leave town. The Abashvili estates are confiscated to make a children's playground and Grusha is divorced because her case is deliberately muddled up with that of the old couple. All celebrate with a dance, and the Singer reports that Azdak disappeared that day and was never seen again. His time is remembered as a golden age that was almost just. Left alone the Singer points the moral: children and valleys should belong to those who care for them best.

Commentary

Structure

The *Caucasian Chalk Circle* was first published in 1949 in the form of a prologue and five acts. It was re-published in 1954 in six acts (called scenes in the present translation). Since 'prologue' is a convenient designation for 'The Struggle for the Valley' it has been used throughout this introduction. The renumbering of the scenes was done before Brecht's production opened at the Berliner Ensemble and was probably prompted by a try-out of the production on 15 June 1954, though many commentators have assumed that it was a defensive response to the poor critical reception of the prologue at the premiere, or even to its omission from the first West German production in 1955. While the play was still in rehearsal Brecht had tried to allay his publisher's misgivings about the kolchos scene:

> 'That the prologue displeases you I don't quite understand, it was the first bit I wrote in the States. The questions posed by the parable must be seen to derive from the necessities of reality, and I think this has been done with an amusing and light touch. Without the prologue it is not evident why the play has not remained the 'Chinese Chalk Circle' (with the old judge's verdict) nor why it is called Caucasian . . . For the dramatisation I needed an historical, explanatory background.' (Letter to Peter Suhrkamp, May, 1954)

This makes it clear that far from being an afterthought — tacked on, it was even suggested, to please his political masters — the prologue was part of Brecht's original conception, and its function was to anchor Grusha's story in reality by relating it to the present. The parable has many fairy-tale elements: the daring escape from the Ironshirts, the miraculous crossing of the broken bridge, the 'dead' husband who recovers, the last-minute re-appointment of the 'good-bad judge' and, of course a wicked mother and a good stepmother. These traditional roles are reversed to demonstrate that society is a better place when rights are earned rather than simply inherited. In addition to this there is running through the play the conviction that a revolution is needed. This implies a Marxist interpretation of history, so that the action is not only seen from the viewpoint of the people, which is the usual fairy-tale perspective, but is also given a socialist dimension. Brecht was evidently not content with this, and one can see that without the prologue, and therefore without the discussion of the need to subject the law to critical scrutiny, the play might easily become simply the story of the trials and final triumph of Grusha. This is why Brecht resorts to the fiction of having 'The Chalk Circle' acted by communists for communists in conjunction with a discussion of the rights to the exploitation of natural resources. This unites the fairy-tale view of the past with an apparently realistic but in fact utopian vision of the present.

There are two versions of 'The Struggle for the Valley', both written in 1944. The first was set in a Caucasian Valley on 7 June 1934 and the irrigation project emanated from a girl who has come back to the valley after being educated in a state agricultural college. The technicalities of agricultural restructuring in the Soviet Union at that time were somewhat remote by the end of the war, so in his second version Brecht not only simplified and generalised the arguments about land utilisation, he brought them up to date by moving the time to the aftermath of the Nazi occupation in 1944 and introducing the theme of post-war reconstruction. The later version is lighter and more humorous in tone and links easily with the ancient play that follows, even though there is a perceptible shift of key. Many productions exploit this by having the kolchos peasants don their costumes on stage for the ancient play and by reminding the audience at intervals of the two levels of the action.

Justice

Brecht frequently uses court scenes in his plays: there are trials in *The Measures Taken, The Exception and the Rule, The Good Person of Szechwan* to name the main examples, and mock trials in *Man equals Man* and *Mr Puntila and his Man Matti,* but in none of these is the theme of justice as central as it is in *The Caucasian Chalk Circle.* Brecht's view of justice was formed in the Weimar Republic (1918-1933) when an attempt was made after the collapse of the monarchy at the end of the Great War to turn Germany into a liberal, parliamentary democracy. The attempt failed and the Weimar Republic was brushed aside by Hitler's fascist Third Reich in 1933. One of the reasons for this failure was that the Weimar Republic took over the administrative apparatus that had served the Kaiser without any attempt at screening or selection, and this meant that the civil service and the judiciary were largely conservative and hostile to the new state. This was particularly clear in the courts' treatment of political offenders. Between 1918 and 1922 for example, of twenty-two assassinations attributable to the left, seventeen received stiff sentences, ten killers being executed. Of 354 murders committed by right-wing extremists only one was rigorously punished and even that not by the death penalty. The average sentence for left-wing offenders was fifteen years; that for the right, four months. Under the Nazis the justice meted out by the People's Court was a travesty, subject to the whim of the Party and ultimately the Führer, Hitler. Brecht knew this only at second-hand, but he never forgot the sight of the police firing on an unarmed workers' demonstration on May Day 1929.

This 'class justice' — the term became an emotive slogan at the time — corroborated the Marxist view of the law as part of the social superstructure, ostensibly a public institution serving all, but in fact a device to protect the interests of the 'ruling classes' (another favourite slogan of the times) and to blunt people's awareness of the injustices of capitalist society. In other words 'ruling-class' law was there to keep the poor in their place and protect the property of the rich. The Azdak scenes in *The Caucasian Chalk Circle* demonstrate that within this framework justice for the poor can only occur in exceptional circumstances, whereas the prologue in Soviet Georgia is intended to show justice as it should be in an ideal world, that is, the direct expression of the people's will to implement the general good.

Brecht acknowledged two sources, one Chinese, the other biblical. The former was a thirteenth-century play by Li Hsing Dao which was widely staged in Germany in 1925 as *The Chalk Circle* in a free adaptation by Klabund. It involved legal action over a disputed child who is first awarded by a false judge after the appropriate bribe to the false claimant who needs him to validate her claim to her dead husband's estate. In a retrial this verdict is overturned by the new Emperor, who awards the child to its real mother. The Emperor is sure of his facts since he himself fathered the child upon the prostitute Haitan before succeeding to the throne. Here the first verdict and the corruption are deviations from the norm which is restored by the Emperor who is the guarantor of the law of the land which is identical with justice.

Brecht's other source was the judgment of Solomon (I Kings

3:16-28) in the matter of two mothers who each claim that a live baby is theirs and a dead one the other's. When Solomon calls for a sword to share the two babies equally the real mother relinquishes her claim and is awarded the child. Like the Chinese Emperor, Solomon is presented as a paragon of justice; and truth, justice and the law are seen to be one and the same thing.

In the configuration adopted by Brecht a maverick judge awards the child to the adoptive mother, and in doing so is seen to uphold justice by subverting the law. Feudal Grusinia, like the Weimar Republic — and, Brecht would have us believe, to a greater or lesser degree like all capitalist states — admits of no equation of truth, law and justice.

In Grusinia the *normal* state of affairs is for the judge to be a scoundrel, as the Ironshirts cynically observe (p.72). The weavers hang Judge Orbellani as an enemy of the people, and it is at the sight of his corpse hanging from the gallows that Azdak changes from self-accusation to jubilation in scene 5. Prince Kazbeki is prevented from outright nepotism by the inconvenient escape of the Grand Duke, and it is only this threat to his security that forces him to invite the 'people' to 'elect' his nephew. For his purposes the weavers do not count, but he may need the support of the military so he flatters the Ironshirts by consulting them. Justice is the servant of power, and if his power were unassailable Kazbeki would nominate his own man to see that justice served his interests. As it is, the Ironshirts capriciously overrule his nomination and appoint Azdak, who holds office only as long as the political situation remains unstable. When the Grand Duke is restored at the end of scene 5 Azdak decides to throw himself on the mercy of the new regime, and his servility when Natella Abashvili returns shows how far he will go to save his skin.

That Azdak becomes judge in the first place is clearly a matter of chance, and this fortuitousness is compounded in scene 6 when, for the second time, he is melodramatically reprieved on the brink of execution — this time by the arrival of a despatch rider bringing his reappointment as judge. The Grand Duke is unaware of Azdak's previous appointment and of his revolutionary sympathies, and he is rewarding Azdak for helping him to escape after the Easter revolt, which of course Azdak now bitterly regrets. It takes a series of chances, whims, mistakes and misunderstandings to ensure that the only judge with whom Grusha stands a chance is in office at the right time. (He disappears from the scene immediately after her trial, the Singer tells us, and is lost in the mists of legend.)

While he holds office Azdak is the absolute arbiter of justice and his technique is one of sardonic improvisation. By the end of the first three cases he has personally accumulated 1000 piastres, half the blackmail and a nice little roan horse, but he has also demonstrated that the practice of medicine is a form of extortion and that wealth and leisure have turned Ludovica into a walking crime. In the case of Mother Grusinia, when he welcomes the axe-man Irakli in court without batting an eyelid, he condones the use of violence in redressing the distribution of wealth, yet glosses this over by imposing a comic fine on the farmers for not believing in miracles. While the Singer stresses the view of the people who admire Azdak because they can see that for once the law is on their side, the audience also sees another side of him; his irony, duplicity and venality. Brecht commented on this in his *Journal*:

> so he continues to practise bourgeois law, but in a degenerate, sabotaged form which was subordinated to the absolute selfishness of the judge. (8.5.44)

The use of the term 'bourgeois law' makes it clear that Brecht is thinking in terms of a modern capitalist society, though his play is set in a feudal state. Like his predecessors Azdak continues to take bribes, a reassuring feature for the Abashvili lawyers in the final scene (p.87). He does not of course guarantee results, but he genuinely resents people assuming that they need not pay up, as his altercation with Grusha (p.91) shows.

The ambivalence of Azdak's behaviour is well established before the final scene, as is his capacity for coming up with last-minute, unorthodox but appropriate verdicts. In the case of Grusha it seems clear that he realises that she has no legal claim to the child, and at one point Brecht suggests that his main concern is to prevent Grusha from incriminating herself in court. When the play was in rehearsal Brecht clearly felt that the trial should not become too much of a foregone conclusion and in his production notes he says:

> The Joke is that he [Azdak] decides and judges on the spur of the moment who *now* gets the child, this is where the Governor's Wife goes wrong, for the chalk circle test is a real test, and it is really through it that Azdak decides who is better suited to have the child. (29.4.1954)

Azdak finally decides that the hardships Grusha has shared with

Michael and the sacrifices she has made to bring him up, plus her inability to hurt him entitle her to have the child. Azdak's final deliberate mistake is to divorce Grusha and Yussup instead of the old couple, thus bringing Grusha and Simon together in a fairy-tale ending. Brecht does not usually tie up the ends like this, let alone finish on such an idyllic note, and James K. Lyon has speculated that Brecht may have been influenced by the fact that he was writing for Broadway.

Grusha

The *Caucasian Chalk Circle* was written after Brecht discussed the project with Luise Rainer, an Austrian actress who had achieved stardom in Hollywood and won two Academy Awards for her film roles, one of them in the film of Pearl S. Buck's novel *The Good Earth*, itself set in China. The idea was that she would play the lead, and she accordingly used her connections to get Brecht a Broadway contract and an $800 advance for the unwritten play. Brecht notes in his *Journal* as he wrote the play that his contractual obligations restricted his artistic freedom, and nine days after finishing the first version he had become dissatisfied with the way Grusha had turned out. Lion Feuchtwanger, a collaborator from Brecht's Munich days who was also an exile in California, confirmed his misgivings. He found Grusha too full of the milk of human kindness. Brecht then spent three weeks rewriting the role. Grusha's ostensible good deeds were not, at least in the first instance, to be the result of positive characteristics like inherent goodness, or incorruptibility, or staunch proletarian defiance, but of servility, lethargy and pig-headedness. Brecht was in fact encountering the problem that arose when *Mother Courage and her Children* was first performed, namely the difficulty of preventing audiences from identifying with mother-figures. The part of Grusha may have suffered at first from being conceived as a Broadway vehicle for a Hollywood star, but at the revision stage Brecht fixed on an image for Grusha which was the antithesis of glamour. Grusha was to be like Dull Gret, the blank-faced woman in an apron and armour who charges through Hell, sword in hand, in Pieter Brueghel's painting *Dulle Griet* (1562) (see page x). This woman was a beast of burden, and around this combination of quixotic audacity and gormlessness Brecht's ideas for redrafting Grusha crystallized. Grusha was to bear the stamp of the backwardness of her class and be 'in a sense a tragic figure, "The Salt of the Earth" (*Journal*, 15.6.1944). Grusha is naive and girlish when we see Simon pulling her leg in their first scene together. Then, when Simon is commanded out of town after the palace revolt, he comes to propose to her, and the love-scene, though convincing, is cool. Brecht avoids intimacy by letting the pair speak in the third person, and they appraise one another quite objectively, like cautious parents arranging a suitable match, though Grusha's final, lyrical speech makes their engagement binding and dignified. When Grusha is left with the Governor's baby in her arms in the chaos that follows, she is the one person on the stage who is oblivious to the danger this involves, though the cook tells her in no uncertain terms that she cannot afford to be her usual dim-witted, easily put-upon self at a time like this, when everybody, servants and masters alike, has to think of saving his own skin. Grusha is a 'born sucker', an Americanism Brecht favoured, who stubbornly persists in seeing the infant Michael as a 'human being' in need. Even so, she resists the temptation to rescue him and sits with him through the night after she has seen his father's head impaled on the city gate. Only in the morning, with a sigh (of resignation?), does she steal off with him like a thief into the dawn without uttering a word. It is left to the Singer to make it clear that this is not a maternal, but a humane response, and to be humane is to ignore your personal or class interest and expose yourself to danger, so Brecht tells us again and again in his plays. This is the sense of the Singer's paradoxical pronouncement, 'Terrible is the temptation to do good!' Grusha responds to the child's plight and yields to temptation, but there is no word to indicate a wish at this point to mother him.

The flight to the Northern Mountains gradually binds her to the child while demanding constant sacrifices of her. When people are defending their own interests, she discovers how adamant (e.g. the old man who charges an inflated price for his milk), ruthless (e.g. aristocratic ladies at the caravansary who think any servant masquerading as an aristocrat must be bent on robbery and murder), and cowardly (e.g. the comfortable, Christian peasant woman who hysterically betrays the baby to the Ironshirts at the first hint of danger) they can be. Grusha copes with these problems and learns from them. When she sees the kind-looking woman on the farm and smells the milk, she thinks she has found a foster mother and can go back and start her own life again, though her relief, as the musician tells us, is tinged with regret.

Grusha now proves to be far more capable than her first scenes would lead us to suspect. The girl who fell so readily for Simon's

innocent teasing now faces up to the leering Corporal. Her
absent-mindedness in the revolt scene is replaced by constructive
urgency as she tries to persuade the peasant woman to lie to the
Ironshirts, and finally knocks out the Corporal when there is no
other way. Yet it is only after twenty-two more days on the road
that she decides to be the child's mother. Brecht saw her
reasonable hesistancy and gradual acceptance of him as evidence of
her suitability as a mother, but even here it is not an emotional
urge that moves Grusha so much as a rueful recognition that they
have been through too much together to part; she changes him into
rags and baptises him, as it were, into her own class. We can,
incidentally, see Grusha's actions as practical Christianity which
contrasts with the lip-service paid to religion by Natella Abashvili
(whom we first see on the way to church) and the righteous
Sister-in-Law. Grusha finally saves the child by taking his and her
own life into her hands and crossing the dangerous bridge.

The actress who played Grusha in the Berliner Ensemble
production decided in rehearsals to make her bundle smaller from
scene to scene in the flight to the Northern Mountains on the
assumption that Grusha would discard soiled clothing as she went
along. Brecht queried this and insisted that she make the bundle
larger because there was no reason to assume that Grusha would
not steal as she went along. This is a useful sidelight on Brecht's
anti-romantic scepticism about his own characters, a scepticism he
wanted the audience to share, and on his willingness to include
visual touches in the interests of complexity of characterisation,
even though, as in this case, the audience might not spot them.

At this stage Grusha still imagines she will be safe with her
brother, but he has a wife who is too respectable to harbour an
unmarried mother. So Grusha learns another lesson: to survive
one has to be clever and cunning, rather than either brave, as she
fears Simon might be, or humane, as she herself initially was. But
to be clever at this stage is to enter into a sham marriage, and
Grusha now realises what a price she is having to pay for being a
fool on Easter Day in Nukha, a price which escalates when her
'dying' husband proves to have been shamming illness to avoid
recruitment. By responding to social pressures to find a regular
home for Michael, Grusha has effectively, and for all she knows
permanently, terminated her own future, which should have
been as a wife to Simon. Motherhood as practised by Grusha is
not an instinctive bond but a willingness to provide, whatever
the cost.

Brecht tries, in a comment on the play, to relate Grusha's story to the story of the collective farmers by introducing the concept of productivity. Grusha's productivity as a 'mother', the part of herself that she invests in Michael, destroys her own private life, whereas the decision that the fruit farmers shall have the valley leads to the most productive use of the land, and contributes to the general welfare because the social system in Soviet Georgia is designed to that end. Productivity as a basis for comparison sits uneasily on Grusha's experiences, but the term does show the stress Brecht sets on the way Grusha fulfils the practical role of a mother, ministering personally to the child's needs. The case he makes might stand up in court today, where the welfare of the child is the prime consideration, at least in Britain, when a natural parent seeks to reclaim a child from long-standing foster-parents.

The experienced Grusha, who has performed the duties of a wife for Yussup for a year while refusing to consummate the marriage, proves in the final scene to have reached a position that has much in common with that of the renegade intellectual Azdak. Her claim to Michael is based on what she has done to bring him up as a useful member of society. Her impetuous diatribe against the corruption of the court strikes a sympathetic chord in the judge, who beams and taps his gavel in time to her words. He sees in her a microcosm of the revolution in practice, and though she cannot find an answer when he asks if she would not like Michael to be rich, he and the Singer know how to interpret her silence. Wealth and power corrupt; so it is a positive gesture, so long as the system based on wealth and power cannot be eradicated, to save one individual from corruption. According to the Singer, this is what Grusha seems intuitively to grasp.

By the time the test takes place, Grusha has proved her worth, and when she cannot bring herself to pull the child apart, the practical mother has become the emotional mother, and the only adequate ending is for Azdak to conjure his solution out of the air.

Azdak

The role of the judge is already crucial in the Chinese *Chalk Circle;* and Brecht's first published variation on the theme, the *Augsburg Chalk Circle (Short Stories 1921-1946,* pp.188-200), introduces in Ignaz Dollinger, who is 'famed throughout Swabia for his boorishness and erudition', a judge with a robust contempt for convention. When he came to write *The Caucasian Chalk Circle* Brecht felt that just to show a judge who was prepared to cut legal corners in the interests of justice was not enough. If his actions were to be more than judicial anarchism they had to emanate from positive elements in Azdak's understanding of society. He wrote in his *Journal*:

> the difficulties of creating the figure of Azdak held me up for two weeks, until i discovered the social cause of his behaviour. at first all i had was his appalling performance as a judge, which resulted in the poor getting off rather lightly. i knew that what i had to show was not just that the law as it stands has to be twisted if justice is to be done in the end, but that something emerges that is to the advantage of those who really need justice when the law is practised in a casual, ignorant, downright bad manner. so Azdak had to have selfish, amoral, parasitic traits and be the lowest, most decrepit judge imaginable. but i still needed a basic cause of a social nature. i found it in his disappointment that the fall of the old rulers did not usher in a new age, merely an age of new masters, so that he goes on dispensing bourgeois justice, but a debased, sabotaged form of bourgeois justice which had been subordinated to the absolute selfishness of the person doing the judging. (8.5.44)

Brecht believed that actions were determined by social rather than pyschological factors, and thus imputes Azdak's erratic behaviour to his disillusionment when the upheaval in Nukha turns out to be an aristocratic coup, rather than a proletarian revolution along the lines of the Persian revolution forty years earlier in his song (p.66). So Azdak, in feudal Georgia, is equipped with a Marxist view of the world which would be more appropriate in pre-revolutionary Russia. One could argue that Azdak's behaviour in his first scene, with the fugitive and Shauva, is as anarchic as later, though he may not know then that the 'revolution' has even taken place, far less failed. This would be to quibble, for what Brecht has done here is to create a figure who has to respond in public life to the same pressures as bedevil Grusha's private life. Azdak is quick and cerebral, where Grusha is slow on the uptake and intuitive; so it's Azdak who exposes the mechanism of society, thus making a link with the collective farmers of the first scene, who also have a social decision to take.

It is an apparent contradiction when Brecht stipulates in his casting notes that only an actor capable of playing a 'totally pure man' should play Azdak, since Azdak is 'a wholly pure man, a disappointed revolutionary who adopts the role of a scoundrelly rogue much as the wise men in Shakespeare play fools'. In a certain sense Brecht's analogy is illuminating. When Azdak indicts the aristocratic generals' mismanagement of the war in the mock trial in scene 5, he is, for the moment, a licensed fool like the one in *King Lear* and can afford to speak home truths. There is much of the jester in his handling of the court cases brought before him. Azdak like Shakespeare's fools speaks, perversely, with the voice of sanity in a world that is out of joint. Yet the application of the concept of purity to Azdak causes problems, for Azdak is too cynical and opportunistic, even too unhygienic, and his shift from defiant jubilation to servility at his first meeting with the Ironshirts is too crass for us to be able to accept him as a pure man in any normal sense (although even non-Marxists have to agree that every scene ultimately demonstrates that his heart is in the right place).

Brecht's theoretical reflections on Azdak must be measured against the figure that the audience sees on the stage, or the reader in his mind's eye, and it is worth noting, that, though Brecht found the judge who is called upon the evaluate the rival claims of two mothers to one child in his sources, both the developing character of Grusha and the vital, unconventional and totally fortuitous judge are wholly his own creations and quite different from the figures in the Chinese original or in Klabund's *Chalk Circle*. Azdak is a commanding figure from his first appearance when he is more than a match for the scared, shambling, fugitive Grand Duke, whom he tutors in the art of proletarian eating, or for the ineffectual policeman Shauva, who comes to arrest him for poaching; but the most telling action in this scene is Azdak's refusal to hand the fugitive over to Shauva, even when he discovers that he is a landowner. His unwillingness to treat an individual simply as a class enemy contrasts directly with the instant hostility of the ladies in the caravansary when they spot Grusha's worker's hands. Azdak is too alienated from the system ever to turn anyone over to the law. Why then does he himself surrender in the next scene? By this time he has discovered from a paper left in his hut that he has harboured the deposed Grand Duke, but more importantly he has heard of the turmoil in the capital and assumes that the revolution he has been waiting for has taken place. As he explains to the uncomprehending Shauva, they are now living in a post-revolutionary age, a utopia where police will be unnecessary, and criminals, if they exist at all, since the social conditions that engender crime will become a thing of the past, will hand themselves over to the people's justice. In the ideal state justice will be self-regulating and identical with the will of the people. The contrast with the situation that faces Azdak when he becomes judge could not be starker, though the audience has already seen this ideal system in action in the 'Struggle for the Valley'.

When Azdak discovers that there has been no revolution he instantly adopts a pose of cowardice, blames the Persian song on his stupid, ignorant grandfather and protests that he did after all personally facilitate the Grand Duke's escape. At the end of this scene when his life is again threatened, he tells Shauva he will 'give no man the pleasure of seeing human greatness' (p.82). So Azdak, though a political idealist, is a cynic when it comes to heroism and a tactician in life for whom self-preservation is paramount. His instant yet calculated responses seem contradictory and paradoxical, nowhere more so than in his court cases. Where Grusha is all on the surface and her motives are even interpreted for the audience by the Singer, Azdak's quirky and amusing behaviour only reveals its meaning to close scrutiny. This starts with the mock trial where his revolutionary analysis of the role of the aristocrats in the war is a repetition of the opinions in the Persian song which almost had him hanged earlier, now cunningly slanted to get the Ironshirts on his side. This time, by contrast, the Ironshirts use the power which the escape of the Grand Duke has temporarily given them to make Azdak judge. The verdicts in the matters of the Invalid and the Blackmailer are another case in point. The court takes half the proceeds to keep the victim's name secret, which is ironically why the landowner paid up in the first place. A malicious view would be that this makes Azdak an accomplice. The Invalid is fined 1000 piastres and the Doctor acquitted of 'an inexcusable professional mistake'. This is a paradoxical verdict. It works on the stage as farce, but the farce has method in it as Azdak's remark to the Blackmailer that he should study medicine shows. His aptitude can only lie in his skill in extracting money, precisely what the doctor has failed to do when he operated on the Limping Man who is, significantly, in rags. So Brecht here equates the professional man with the blackmailer, just as he equated the bourgeoisie with robbers in *The Threepenny Opera*. The monied classes, the Landowner and the Invalid end up poorer, whereas the haphazard Doctor gets off free. Underlying the knockabout farce and the Judge's witty summing up there is a vision of a society where medicine will be a service to the community and not a marketable product, but this is concealed behind the apparent whimsy of the action.

Azdak is a drunkard. He is tipsy when he first appears, he regales himself with wine during the trial of Mother Grusinia, and after the Ironshirts have manhandled him he swigs a jug of sweet red wine before he can face Grusha's case. He is insistently vulgar. Here too there is a pattern. He rebukes the Grand Duke for his messy eating, but this appears to be more for his blatant greediness than for his manners. Yet here again paradox reigns, for Azdak calls the Grand Duke an 'arse-hole' and a 'sow', and his kind 'well -born stinkers'. For the Servant at the caravansary the upper classes are people who can't wipe their own arses (p.32), and in the Persian song the rulers are 'incapable of letting down their own trousers' (p.66). When Natella Abashvili appears, she complains that the smell of the common people always gives her migraine (p.85). This anal imagery runs through the play. The aristocrats with their detachment from natural functions and their sensitive noses are stinkers to Azdak and the lower orders, but the odour they exude is metaphorical, the stench of exploitation. It is not surprising among these odours that Azdak as Judge occasionally has to nip out and smell a rose to establish a standard for himself (p.91).

It is much the same with appearances. The aristocrats are distinguished by their fine apparel. The poor are in rags. Azdak in the preamble to the mock trial claims that the law is injured if the Judge is not wearing the appropriate paraphernalia in a seemly manner (p.69), yet he himself displays his tattered underwear in court (p.92). Fine clothes and formality, like fine manners, this implies, are the prerogative of the ruling classes and therefore tainted. Azdak's vulgarity is an affirmation of his solidarity as a bourgeois intellectual with the poor and an assertion that the attributes of poverty have their own dignity.

Finally one should not overlook Azdak's extrovert theatricality which injects vitality into the play as soon as he appears and makes him a rewarding part for a character actor. He is one of nature's incurables, a slave to the gab, a joker and a judge, an immoralist and amateur politician, a chameleon who will wear whatever face the situation will bear. By the end of the play, with the full restoration of the old regime imminent, things are too hot for him and, like the mythical gunslingers who imposed law on the Wild West, when his work is done and every issue resolved he disappears and leaves the other characters to make a dancing exit.

Epic theatre

The literary term 'epic' is traditionally applied to forms of writing in which the author recounts a story, using as many episodes and characters as a comprehensive account of his subject demands. In modern times the epic has been the preserve of prose fiction, and its standard form the novel. The term 'dramatic' is traditionally applied to forms of writing intended for performance, and these are limited in number of characters and settings by the conventions and resources of the theatre, and in length by the audience's patience and concentration, so that dramatists are in practice restricted to presenting a concentrated plot which shows a conflict and its resolution. The term 'epic theatre', which was first used in Germany in the 1920's and has become firmly associated with the name of Brecht, cuts across the traditional divisions. Epic story-telling is objective; the author stands back from his story as he tells it, and he may interpolate his own comment on events. It was the objectivity and the simultaneous scope for comment in epic writing that attracted the dramatist Brecht, and the beginning of epic theatre coincide with German experiments in the use of the theatre as an instrument of political instruction.

From the beginning of his career Brecht had fought a running battle against the conventional theatre of his day which he dismissed as 'culinary', since, like expert cooking, it delighted the senses without impinging on the mind. Banners in the auditorium for the production of one of his first plays, *Drums in the Night* in 1922, told the audience not to 'gawp so romantically', and in his essay *On Experimental Theatre* (1939) Brecht asked,

> How can the theatre be entertaining and at the same time instructive? How can it be taken out of the traffic in intellectual drugs and transformed from a place of illusion to a place of insight?

For Brecht the traditional, or dramatic theatre was a place where the audience were absorbed into a comforting illusion which played on their emotions and left them drained, but with a sense of satisfaction which predisposed them to accept the world as they found it. What he himself was looking for was a theatre that would help to change the world.

He first tabulated his ideas on epic theatre in his *Notes on the Opera 'The Rise and Fall of the City of Mahoganny'* (1930) where he set out the contrasts between the dramatic theatre and the epic theatre in a list.

DRAMATIC THEATRE	EPIC THEATRE
plot	narrative
implicates the spectator in a stage situation	turns the spectator into an observer, but
wears down his capacity for action	arouses his capacity for action
provides him with sensations	forces him to take decisions
experience	picture of the world
the spectator is involved in something	he is made to face something
suggestion	argument
instinctive feelings are preserved	brought to the point of recognition
the spectator is in the thick of it, shares the experience	the spectator stands outside, studies
the human being is taken for granted	the human being is the object the inquiry
he is unalterable	he is alterable and able to alter
eyes on the finish	eyes on the course
one scene makes another	each scene for itself
growth	montage
linear development	in curves
evolutionary determinism	jumps
man as a fixed point	man as a process
thought determines being	social being determines thought
feeling	reason

(from *Brecht on Theatre*, p. 37)

The first change of emphasis Brecht advocated was in the manner in which events were presented to the audience. Dramatic theatre enacted plots, involved the audience and stimulated their emotions only to dissipate this active response. Epic theatre was to tell a story in a way that invited the audience to consider the events involved and then to make their own assessment of them. To achieve this, adjustments had to be made to the form of the play. The dramatic play was a closed system of interdependent scenes, each one evolving inexorably from its predecessor, but with the plot so structured that the audience was kept in suspense, wondering how it would all end. The epic play was to be assembled as a montage of independent incidents which showed a process taking place; it would move from scene to scene by curves and jumps, which would keep the audience alert to the way in which things were happening, so that they would finally be able, would indeed be compelled, to judge whether that was the right way. Brecht sometimes compared his plays to scientific experiments; specimens of human behaviour were subjected to scrutiny to see what principles governed them and whether these principles could be improved. Change for the better lay at the centre of Brecht's thinking, and this meant altering the classical notion that the hero of a play should be a fixed character. The conflict between such immutable 'Characters' and their world was the stuff of traditional drama, but Brecht rejected the notion that human nature was fixed, and that man's own thinking governed his being, in favour of a concept of human nature as capable of change. In epic theatre man's thinking is conditioned by his social situation and will change if that changes. At the same time he is the agent of social change, so that there is a constant dialectic, or process of reciprocal influence and change.

Grusha is a case in point. The Cook warns her in the chaos after the revolt that it is no time to be soft and obliging, but she still succumbs to the temptation to do good and rescues the Governor's abandoned child. This is the start of a sequence of events that teach her what it means to fend for herself in a competitive society, changing her in the process from a thoughtless, willing servant with a streak of stubbornness into a class-conscious worker whose sense of outrage at the apparent corruption of Azdak's court procedure finally explodes, rashly be it said, into an indictment of the class society.

The Caucasian Chalk Circle is a refined and complex example of epic theatre. It does not develop a conflict in terms of character, but tells two separate though convergent tales from ancient Grusinia which are enacted because they have some bearing on the realistic prologue set in Soviet Georgia which precedes them. The first abrupt shift, from a scene which has distinct features of Socialist Realism with its Girl Tractor Driver and its good-natured 'shop-floor' argument about future policy, to a scene in which the workers appear as their own feudal forbears, some of them opulently dressed and masked, is anti-illusionistic. Even in the television age, when the flashback has become a standard feature of our visual syntax, the way the Azdak story at the beginning of the fifth scene reverts back to the very Easter Day on which Grusha's story began can still confuse student readers. These are the large jumps between the separate blocks which make up this 'montage' of stories. The Grusha and Azdak stories are then themselves each assembled from short episodes which illuminate aspects of the characters' interaction with society, and the episodes are linked by the Singer who functions as a narrator and commentator. The constant alternation between two modes of presentation, the multi-character dramatic episodes and the solo narrative, forces the audience to retune at brief intervals and inhibits suspension of disbelief. The episodic structure of the play runs through scenes two to five where Brecht is putting together the characters of the two protagonists bit by bit. The final scene which demonstrates the resolution of a conflict (a feature it shares with the prologue), is, however, predominantly dramatic. The Singer intervenes only once and apart from this he simply opens the scene and then rounds it off by drawing the moral.

The use of the Singer as a narrator in *The Caucasian Chalk Circle* merits close attention as the most consistent and at the same time most varied use of this epic device in all Brecht's plays. We know at the start of the Grusha story that the Singer is the celebrated folk-singer Arkady Cheidze who is staging the two plays within the play. He indicates his status as prompter and stage-manager by leafing through a dog-eared script (p.9) to refresh his memory before launching into his verse description of 'city of the damned', and he stands outside the action from then on, interrupting to link the episodes, to fill in relevant information economically, to comment on the action and keep the audience's assessment on the correct lines, to demonstrate in his own terms what is going through Grusha's mind, and sum up the message at the end. After he has focused our attention on the Governor's visit to church on Easter Sunday, a crowd of beggars and petitioners followed by the Governor's retinue issues from the palace gate and, in a tableau with dialogue, illustrates and expands the narrator's introduction.

This establishes the pattern of epic introduction and dramatic illustration which alternates throughout the play. The audience is first told what is going to happen and is then free to concentrate on how it happens (or so the theory goes), and enough unexplained detail is introduced (the message which the Rider fails to deliver, the curious edginess of the Fat Prince) to keep the audience wondering. With his atmospheric evocation at the end of this first scene ('On the church square the pigeons preen themselves' p.12) the Singer prepares us for the meeting of Grusha and Simon, which is duly acted out. Then he moves the story on by reporting the coup that has taken place offstage, which lends dramatic irony to the following scene depicting the Governor's return from church. At the end of this episode the Singer comments, in a manner that has been compared to the chorus in Greek tragedy, on the *hubris*, or excessive pride of the great; he uses the baroque image of the wheel of fortune, which traditionally symbolises the transience of earthly power and wealth, but turns it into a sign of hope for the people, the kind of revolutionary hope we later see in Azdak. The Singer's commentary is from the beginning sympathetic to the cause of the underdog. In a tableau without dialogue the Governor is now marched on in chains by armed guards. He need give no sign of hearing when the Singer comments ironically on his suddenly reduced needs and prospects, for this is really a polemical intrusion directed at the audience, whose collusion the Singer is seeking. The Singer is now the voice of the people, and, with a further general observation that those who serve the great benefit less from their rule than they suffer from their fall, he introduces a complex episode with the doctors, the servants, the adjutant, and Grusha and Simon which demonstrates the truth of this statement. Finally Grusha is left alone with the choice of taking or leaving the Governor's son, and here Brecht reduces the possibility of emotional involvement by giving Grusha no lines at all and having the Singer mediate her feelings. In this way we are made to see Grusha's gesture as part of a pattern of natural, humane behaviour, like feeling love, or feeling at one with nature, or feeling the simple satisfaction of a task well done. To counteract any notion that maternal feelings might come into it at this stage, the baby's appeal is framed as a series of questions that clarify the implications for Grusha if she ignores him. Using the Singer, Brecht can objectively explore a decision-making process that could otherwise only be revealed by means of the more subjective soliloquy. He can also bring out the dialectic of Grusha's problem, for she loses whichever way she chooses to act, as is indicated by the paradoxical line 'Terrible is the temptation to do good!' (p.25). Through the Singer, Grusha's behaviour is seen as naive and uncorrupted and to that extent positive, though to persist in saving the child in the teeth of all advice is shown to be stubborn and dangerous.

In scene three the voices of the Musicians join that of the Singer to form a two-part commentary. He outlines the action, while they ask — somewhat melodramatically — how Grusha can elude her pursuers. Before the farmhouse scene, they explain that fatigue is now taking its toll and forcing Grusha to abandon the child; after she has left him, the Singer and Musicians take on the role of interviewer and interviewee to express by proxy Grusha's mixed feelings as she walks silently away, again doing what only a potentially sentimental soliloquy could otherwise do. In the fourth scene the Singer again speaks alone as he rehearses in the form of hypothetical dialogue the welcome Grusha expects from her brother, and here the effect is one of contrast, for the actual reception which follows is quite different. For the rest the Singer mainly marks the passage of time in this scene until Simon's return, when it is the Singer who fills in the things the laconic, confused characters leave unsaid: first Simon's war experiences, then Grusha's explanation of her connection with the child. This means that while Simon sees only one thing — Grusha's affirmative answer when the Ironshirts ask if Michael is her child — the audience has a total, yet detached, view of the complexities of the situation.

In the last two scenes the Singer's function changes slightly, because Azdak is articulate enough to speak for himself, and unsavoury and ironic enough to prevent the audience from identifying directly with him. The Singer still provides essential information, dating the encounter with the Fugitive to the Easter Sunday of the palace revolt, and explaining Azdak's change of attitude between that encounter and the next scene by telling us that Azdak now knows that the Fugitive was really the Grand Duke. More characteristic of this phase are his comments on Azdak's career, which he celebrates in the songs he sings with the Musicians on pages 77 and 80. These songs put Azdak's constructive subversion of the legal system into perspective for the audience as a brief interlude of justice for the underdog in an age of exploitation.

At the end of the play it falls to the Singer to make the link between the *Chalk Circle* and the Prologue:

The children to the maternal, that they thrive;
The carriages to the good drivers; that they are driven well;
And the valley to the waterers, that it shall bear fruit.

The principle of social utility, he implies, is at work in the case of Grusha as in the case of the Rosa Luxemburg kolchos.

The songs (not only of the Singer, but of the other characters too) involve a shift in the key of the production, simply by virtue of being sung when all the rest is spoken, and this is usually seen as another alienation effect. But Angelika Hurwicz, who played Grusha in the Berliner Ensemble production, warns interpreters against over-emphasising this. She cites the song which provides the backing for the reunion of Grusha and Simon as an example:

> . . . Brecht wanted the actors to accompany the text sung by the
> Singer with finely modulated facial expressions. Mistrust,
> reproach, disappointment were to be reflected in their faces.
> The song is a poetic interpretation of their silence. At the same
> time the Singer as he expressed Simon Chachava's reproachful
> thoughts was not to sing in a detached narrative fashion, but
> was to be angry and accusing. This moment cannot be
> categorised under any stylistic principle, it is simply a poetic,
> autonomous, artistically beautiful moment.

At moments like this it is apparent that any attempt to codify the
principles of epic theatre and to claim that at a given point they
will operate in a given way fails to take account of Brecht's
personal style and his feeling for the theatre, which were the
ultimate deciding factor in how a particular scene was best
interpreted to preserve the overall artistic unity of the production.

One more detail to illustrate Brecht's pragmatism as a director:
in the fifth scene Azdak was to shave, but Ernst Busch, the actor
playing Azdak, had just done a shaving scene in *Mr Puntila and his
Man Matti*, so Brecht obligingly let him patch his coat instead. It is
not surprising that Brecht rejected as too arty the designation
'dramatist', or 'poet in the theatre' and instead popularised a new
word in German to describe his craft, *'Stückeschreiber'*, which
simply means 'play-writer'.

Staging

In November 1953 Brecht commissioned Karl von Appen to
design the set, costumes and masks for *The Caucasian Chalk Circle*,
and the designer wrote a brief, graphic account of their
collaboration. Brecht first suggested 'Krippenfiguren', the carved
nativity groups that are commonly set up at Christmas in South
German churches, as the optical key to the production. He wanted
a primitive, naive effect. He then decided on the key materials,
which were, as Appen observes, a crucial matter in Brecht's
theatrical practice. The feudal princes were to be characterised by
copper, silver, steel and silks, whereas the people would be dressed
in coarse linen. Wood and leather were also permitted, but the
designer had to confine himself to the use of the prescribed
materials. They also established the historical context. Brecht
claimed, Appen reports wryly, that he used the same technique
with his barber. He would tell him he wanted his hair cut to two

millimetres all over, but apart from that he could cut it in any style he liked. Using the permitted materials, the designer's job was to produce costumes that looked Caucasian, keeping the idea of folk-carvings in mind.

Appen first sketched the groupings for each scene, and from this a basic layout was developed. The stage was enclosed by a semi-circular white backcloth known as a cyclorama, in front of which hung a changeable drop-cloth, or 'flag' as Brecht termed it, painted, as can be seen from the illustrations, in the style of Chinese ink-drawings. Behind this, pieces of scenery could be erected on the revolving stage. During the 'Flight to the Northern Mountains', for example, Grusha plodded with the child on her back against the revolve, and the set for each episode emerged from behind the 'flag', travelled towards her and stopped for her to play the scene. This fluid, mobile staging enabled the many scenes to flow into one another without any waste of time.

The painted drop-cloths and pieces of scenery Appen calls 'quotations', because they presented a selected part which stood for the whole. On the drop-cloth for scene 2 a wedge-shaped beehive of houses represents the city of Nukha, and a miniaturised facade on the stage represents the church. While these 'quotations' were part of Brecht's anti-illusionistic, alienating technique, the chosen segments of reality had to have a feel of solid authenticity. This, too, can be seen in the illustrations. The facade of the church with its statues in niches and its domes surmounted by Orthodox crosses was made of papier-mâché covered with silver and copper foil to look like costly beaten metal. Brecht and Appen had a contest at devising props, the idea being that each one should tell something about its owner and be a museum piece in its own right.

Angelika Hurwicz makes the following comment on the effort Brecht lavished on the optical effect of his plays:

> The set, though quite unnaturalistic, was finished in great detail. Brecht also drew pictures to describe the environment and the external appearance of his characters. In these pictures he was as explicit as a novelist. This is as much of a reason for calling his theatre 'epic theatre' as the non-existent special style of acting for which it is usually so named.

It was decided, partly because the large number of parts in the play made doubling inevitable, that masks would be used to differentiate the characters, and a range of masking was used, with the good characters appearing simply in make-up ('mask' is in fact the German term for theatrical make-up), while the feudal aristocrats had their faces frozen, as it were, in full-face masks, with their lackeys, the doctors and lawyers, wearing half-masks.

As was usual in the Berliner Ensemble productions, the lighting throughout was a constant cool white.

Language

The language of *The Caucasian Chalk Circle* has attracted relatively little comment, despite its variety of texture and pattern. The play moves easily from the down-to-earth exchanges of the kolchos peasants to the insincere artificialities of the Nukha court circle and back to the bantering directness of Grusha and Simon. The Governor's Wife has her own upper-class tone and mannerisms which are instantly recognizable when Grusha mimics them in scene 3 (pp.28-30). An even more personal style is that of the fugitive Grand Duke whose short sentences without pronouns Azdak deftly apes in scene 5. When the Nephew lapses into this 'jerky, clipped manner of speech' (p.72) it becomes clear that parody of an authoritarian speech pattern is intended. (Prussian artistocrats may have been curt like this, but in English it is more characteristic of N.C.O's than of officers and gentlemen, and not at all of royalty.) Simon Chachava also has a style of his own with a predilection for proverbial pronouncements which culminates in his verbal duel with Azdak (p.91), who for his part has the most trenchant and witty style of all. There are biblical echoes like the Ironshirt's 'hollow reed or a tinkling cymbal' (p.32), there are ballads ('no more did the lower orders . . . p.77), there are folk-songs ('He who wears the shoes of gold' p.93) and there are heartfelt personal lyrics ('Go calmly into the battle, soldier' p.19). This is a poetic play, linguistically finely wrought, and a good example of how Brecht used language to encapsulate the 'gestus' or characteristic presence of his stage figures.

Music

The music for *The Caucasian Chalk Circle* by Paul Dessau was written for a nine-piece orchestra, using on occasion a piano prepared with drawing-pins as its hammers and a specially constructed set of gongs. Dessau composed 42 separate pieces which indicates how important the music is for the overall effect of the play. Some pieces are simple and melodic, like the accompaniment to Grusha's first song (p.19) while others like the Singer's commentary on Grusha's decision to take the child (pp.24-25) are technically demanding. The music for scene 4, 'In the Northern Mountains' which reflects the new locality with a change in quality is based on a book of folk-dances from Azerbaijan, and indeed much of the music has a folk quality about it. Dessau suggests that it should be possible for musicians of modest accomplishment to cope with his score and implies that school or college productions should keep the music in. With regard to the episode when Grusha decides to save the child he makes the following comment on the dramatic function of the music:

> This important piece is difficult and if the Singer is not up to it the words must be spoken. (They can be spoken to the music.) Grusha does what the Singer says, exactly as he describes it. (This is a borrowing from the Chinese theatre which Brecht frequently used later.) Remember how much a talented and ambitious performer can learn from the polyrhythmic music for the mime sequence here.

Meaning

In a sense the meaning of *The Caucasian Chalk Circle* is obvious. Brecht even sums it up for us through his Singer in the last four lines of the play:

> That what there is shall belong to those who are good for it, thus
> The children to the maternal, that they thrive;
> The carriages to good drivers, that they are driven well;
> And the valley to the waterers, that it shall bear fruit.

Grusha will be good for Michael, just as the fruit-farming kolchos (collective) will be good for the valley, and thus the two parts of the play are united in a utilitarian conclusion.

This is fine as far as it goes, but it sheds little light on the social and political implications of what is clearly a political play. It was written in 1944 when Hitler's armies were on the retreat on all fronts, and Brecht was beginning to look beyond the defeat of fascism to the future, a communist future in which his faith remained unshaken, despite his knowledge of Stalinism or, more pertinently in the context of the play, of the atrocities associated with the collectivisation of agriculture in the USSR. The first scene is set in the Soviet Union. It alludes to the Russian people's sufferings at the hands of the Germans and shows the restored Soviet system working smoothly, too smoothly Western critics thought when the play was performed by the Berliner Ensemble in 1954. The director of the West German premiere at Frankfurt in 1955 omitted the first scene as being politically inopportune at that stage in the Cold War. Besides being thought propagandistic, the prologue was deemed to be drab, undramatic and scarcely relevant. Without it the play was more poetic, it was felt. Eastern critics tended to accept the prologue as an act of homage to the Soviet Union, though Soviet commentators were later to point out that the procedure it shows bears little resemblance to the real process of decision-taking on collective farms. The play then touched a nerve, at least in West Germany, in the fifties, but time has blunted that particular effect. Recently an American scholar, Betty Nance Weber, has tried to reveal a hidden meaning by showing that the events of Easter Day and after in Grusinia can be made to match up with the early history of the Soviet Union. This attempt to repoliticise the play in concrete historical terms does not really work. It is now broadly accepted that the first scene is an integral part of the play, and any interpretation of the play must explain the connection between the prologue and the interlocking Grusha and Azdak stories.

Brecht himself is not entirely helpful in his comments on this. He calls *The Caucasian Chalk Circle* a 'parabolic play' in a letter to his publisher, Peter Suhrkamp, in May 1954, but in his notes on the play he later claims that 'The Chalk Circle' is a story in its own right which proves nothing in relation to the prologue, but merely demonstrates 'a certain type of wisdom that might serve as an example for the case in hand'. It is in fact difficult to find in the 'ancient play' anything that would help the collective farmers. There are thematic links; shared hardships bring Grusha and Michael together, just as the shared hardships of the resistance draw the two kolchoses together. The goat breeders relinquish land to which they have a legal title, just as the natural mother loses her legitimate child. In Grusinia however Natella Abashvili's legal claim to the child is nullified as part of Azdak's entertaining judicial improvisations which make the law more arbitrary and much more unpredictable than even his predecessors' while cunningly loading the dice in favour of the poor. There is nothing for the peasants to learn from Azdak's procedure, either as actors while they perform this *Lehrstück* (learning play) or as spectators. What they can learn is how unjust conditions in the bad old days were, and how in those days it took a miracle for a 'poor old body' to get a ham, and two miraculous flukes for a revolutionary judge to be in office when he is needed.

Brecht grafted on to his judge an anachronistic revolutionary consciousness which was in none of his models. Azdak knows that the system needs to be changed, and all he can do is to find ways round it, but this in itself is a practical demonstration in adverse political circumstances of what the Girl Tractor Driver means when she says, 'The laws will have to be re-examined to see whether they are still valid' (p.5). To be valid they must serve the broad interests of the people. In the prologue this is seen to be happening in a simple form of consultation as the peasants determine the utilisation of the land in the valley and thus their own future, whereas 'The Chalk Circle' shows how difficult it was in feudal (and by extension capitalist) times to achieve the same end.

It might of course be said to be paradoxical that in creating the vital, unruly, anarchic, individualist Azdak, from whom justice briefly flows, Brecht has produced the antithesis, if not the anathema of the faceless bureaucrats who, since he wrote, have come to seem characteristic of the new ruling classes in east and west in the post-war era. It might also be said that a scene in which the collective peasants make their own reasoned decision which is then reported back to the capital in good faith by the strikingly docile Expert is the work of a political dreamer, unaware of the complexities (or realities) of modern society. But Brecht was well aware of these complexities, so perhaps he is telling his audience that they, the people, are the final arbiters of the validity of the law and of their own destiny, and it is for them to ensure that their rights are not usurped by judges, or bureaucrats acting in their name.

Further reading

Bertolt Brecht: *Brecht on Theatre* (translation and notes by John Willett), Eyre Methuen, London, 1964. Brecht's essential theoretical and critical writings assembled in one handy volume

Graham Bartram and Anthony Waine: *Brecht in Perspective*, Longman, London and New York, 1982. Essays by British scholars which examine Brecht's literary, historical and social background, relate him to the German theatrical tradition, and compare him with seminal figures like Piscator and Stanislavsky.

Keith A. Dickson: *Towards Utopia*, Oxford University Press, 1978. Closely argued study of Brecht and his work which draws on research in English, German and Russian. Dickson pursues the utopian vision behind Brecht's satirical presentation of life. The book is organized around themes (Man and Society, the Historical Perspective, etc.) and deals with plays, poetry and prose.

Martin Esslin: *Brecht: a Choice of Evils*, 4th ed., Methuen, London, 1984. An early appraisal with useful insights, in spite of the writer's obvious antipathy to Brecht's politics.

Claude Hill: *Bertolt Brecht*, Twayne, Boston, 1975. An American survey, clear and useful, with separate chapters on major works.

James K. Lyon: *Bertolt Brecht in America*, Methuen, London, 1982. Fascinating account of Brecht's U.S. exile with a chapter on the genesis of *The Caucasian Chalk Circle*.

Jan Needle and Peter Thompson: *Brecht*, Blackwell, Oxford, 1981. The authors have studied Brecht in English translation. They are best on the plays in performance.

J.M. Ritchie: *Brecht: Der kaukasische Kreidekreis*, Edward Arnold, London, 1976. A blow-by-blow commentary with titles and quotations in German.

Alfred D. White: *Bertolt Brecht's Great Plays*, Macmillan, London, 1978. Analyses of the major plays in separate chapters.

John Willett: *The Theatre of Bertolt Brecht*, 4th ed., Eyre Methuen, London, 1977. Seminal compendium of basic information.

All Brecht's major plays (and many minor works) are published in English translation in the Methuen Modern Plays series. Also published by Methuen are volumes of Brecht's *Poems 1913-56, Short Stories 1921-46* and *Diaries 1920-22.*

The Caucasian Chalk Circle

Collaborator: R. BERLAU

Translators: JAMES AND TANIA STERN, *with* W. H. AUDEN

Characters

Delegates of the Galinsk goat-breeding kolchos: an old peasant, a peasant woman, a young peasant, a very young workman · Members of the Rosa Luxemburg fruit-growing kolchos: an old peasant, a peasant woman, the agronomist, the girl tractor driver; the wounded soldier and other peasants from the kolchos · The expert from the capital · The singer Arkadi Cheidze · His musicians · Georgi Abashvili, the Governor · His wife, Natella · Their son, Michael · Shalva, the adjutant · Arsen Kazbeki, the fat prince · The rider from the capital · Niko Mikadze and Mikha Loladze, doctors · Simon Chachava, a soldier · Grusha Vachnadze, a kitchen-maid · Three architects · Four chambermaids: Assia, Masha, Sulika and Fat Nina · A nurse · A man cook · A woman cook · A stableman · Servants in the governor's palace · The governor's and the fat prince's Ironshirts and soldiers · Beggars and petitioners · The old peasant with the milk · Two elegant ladies · The innkeeper · The servant · A corporal · 'Blockhead', a soldier · A peasant woman and her husband · Three merchants · Lavrenti Vachnadze, Grusha's brother · His wife, Aniko · Their stableman · The peasant woman, for a time Grusha's mother-in-law · Yussup, her son · Brother Anastasius, a monk · Wedding guests · Children · Azdak, the village clerk · Shauva, a policeman · A refugee, the Grand Duke · The doctor · The invalid · The limping man · The blackmailer · Ludovica, the innkeeper's daughter-in-law · A poor old peasant woman · Her brother-in-law Irakli, a bandit · Three farmers · Illo Shaboladze and Sandro Oboladze, lawyers · The very old married couple

THE STRUGGLE FOR THE VALLEY

Among the ruins of a badly shelled Caucasian village the members of two kolchos villages are sitting in a circle, smoking and drinking wine. They consist mainly of women and old men, but there are also a few soldiers among them. With them is an expert of the State Reconstruction Commission from the capital.

A PEASANT WOMAN *left, pointing:* In those hills over there we stopped three Nazi tanks. But the apple orchard had already been destroyed.

AN OLD PEASANT *right:* Our beautiful dairy farm. All in ruins.

A GIRL TRACTOR DRIVER *left:* I set fire to it, Comrade.
Pause.

THE EXPERT: Now listen to the report: the delegates of the Galinsk goat-breeding kolchos arrived in Nukha. When the Hitler armies were approaching, the kolchos had been ordered by the authorities to move its goat-herds further to the east. The kolchos now considers resettling in this valley. Its delegates have investigated the village and the grounds and found a high degree of destruction. *The delegates on the right nod.* The neighbouring Rosa Luxemburg fruit-growing kolchos—*to the left*—moves that the former grazing land of the Galinsk kolchos, a valley with scanty growth of grass, should be used for the replanting of orchards and vineyards. As an expert of the Reconstruction Commission, I request the two kolchos villages to decide between themselves whether the Galinsk kolchos shall return here or not.

AN OLD MAN *right:* First of all, I want to protest against the restriction of time for discussion. We of the Galinsk kolchos have spent three days and three nights getting here. And now we are allowed a discussion of only half a day.

A WOUNDED SOLDIER *left:* Comrade, we no longer have as many villages and no longer as many working hands and no longer as much time.

THE GIRL TRACTOR DRIVER *left:* All pleasures have to be rationed. Tobacco is rationed, and wine and discussion, too.

THE OLD MAN *right, sighing:* Death to the Fascists! But I will come to the point and explain to you why we want to have our valley back. There are a great many reasons, but I want to begin with one of the simplest. Makinae Abakidze, unpack the goat cheese.

A peasant woman, right, takes from a basket an enormous cheese wrapped in a cloth. Applause and laughter.

Help yourselves, comrades. Start in.

AN OLD PEASANT *left, suspiciously:* Is this meant to influence us, perhaps?

THE OLD MAN *right, amidst laughter:* How could it be meant as an influence, Surab, you valley-thief? Everyone knows that you will take the cheese and the valley, too. *Laughter.* All I expect from you is an honest answer: Do you like the cheese?

THE OLD MAN *left:* The answer is yes.

THE OLD MAN *right:* Oh. *Bitterly.* I might have guessed you know nothing about cheese.

THE OLD MAN *left:* Why not? When I tell you I like it!

THE OLD MAN *right:* Because you can't like it. Because it's not what it was in the old days. And why isn't it? Because our goats don't like the new grass as they used to like the old. Cheese is not cheese because grass is not grass, that's it. Mind you put that in your report.

THE OLD MAN *left:* But your cheese is excellent.

THE OLD MAN *right:* It's not excellent. Barely decent. The new grazing land is no good, whatever the young people may say. I tell you, it's impossible to live there. It doesn't even smell of morning there in the morning.

Several people laugh.

THE EXPERT: Don't mind their laughter. They understand you all the same. Comrades, why does one love one's country? Because the bread tastes better there, the sky is higher, the air smells better, voices sound stronger, the ground is easier to walk on. Isn't that so?

THE OLD MAN *right:* The valley has belonged to us for centuries.

THE SOLDIER *left:* What does that mean—for centuries? Nothing belongs to anyone for centuries. When you were young you didn't even belong to yourself, but to Prince Kazbeki.

THE OLD MAN *right:* According to the law the valley belongs to us.

THE GIRL TRACTOR DRIVER: The laws will have to be re-examined in any case, to see whether they are still valid.

THE OLD MAN *right:* That's obvious. You mean to say it makes no difference what kind of tree stands beside the house where one was born? Or what kind of neighbour one has? Doesn't that make any difference? We want to go back just to have you next door to our kolchos, you valley-thieves. Now you can laugh that one off.

THE OLD MAN *left, laughing:* Then why don't you listen to what your 'neighbour', Kato Vachtang, our agronomist, has to say about the valley?

A PEASANT WOMAN *right:* We haven't said anywhere near all we have to say about our valley. Not all the houses are destroyed. At least the foundation wall of the dairy farm is still standing.

THE EXPERT: You can claim State support—both here and there. You know that.

A PEASANT WOMAN *right:* Comrade Expert, we're not trading now. I can't take your cap and hand you another, and say: 'This one's better.' The other one might be better, but you prefer yours.

THE GIRL TRACTOR DRIVER: A piece of land is not like a cap. Not in our country, comrade.

THE EXPERT: Don't get angry. It's true that we have to consider a piece of land as a tool with which one produces something useful. But it's also true that we must recognize the love for a particular piece of land. Before we continue the discussion I suggest that you explain to the comrades of the Galinsk kolchos just what you intend to do with the disputed valley.

THE OLD MAN *right:* Agreed.

THE OLD MAN *left:* Yes, let Kato speak.

THE EXPERT: Comrade Agronomist!

THE AGRONOMIST *rising. She is in military uniform:* Last winter, comrades, while we were fighting here in these hills as partisans, we discussed how after the expulsion of the Germans we could increase our orchards to ten times their former size. I have prepared a plan for an irrigation project. With the help of a dam on our mountain lake, three hundred hectares of unfertile land can be irrigated. Our kolchos could then grow not only more fruit, but wine as well. The project, however, would pay only if the disputed valley of the Galinsk kolchos could also be included. Here are the calculations. *She hands the expert a briefcase.*

THE OLD MAN *right:* Write into the report that our kolchos plans to start a new stud farm.

THE GIRL TRACTOR DRIVER: Comrades, the project was conceived during the days and nights when we had to take cover in the mountains and often were without ammunition for our few rifles. Even to get a pencil was difficult.

Applause from both sides.

THE OLD MAN *right:* Our thanks to the comrades of the Rosa Luxemburg kolchos and to all those who defended our country.

They shake hands and embrace.

THE PEASANT WOMAN *left:* Our thoughts were that our soldiers—both your men and our men—should return to a still more fertile homeland.

THE GIRL TRACTOR DRIVER: As the poet Mayakovsky said: 'The home of the Soviet people shall also be the home of Reason!'

The delegates on the right (except the old man) have risen and, with the expert, study the agronomist's plans. Exclamations such as: 'Why is there a fall of 66 feet?'—'This rock here is to be dynamited!'—'Actually, all they need is cement and dynamite!'— 'They force the water to come down here, that's clever!'

A VERY YOUNG WORKMAN *right, to the old man, right:* They are going to irrigate all the fields between the hills—look at that, Alleko.

THE OLD MAN *right:* I am not going to look at it. I knew the project would be good. I won't have a revolver pointed at my chest.

THE SOLDIER: But they are only pointing a pencil at your chest.

Laughter.

THE OLD MAN *right. He gets up gloomily and walks over to look at the drawings:* These valley-thieves know only too well that we can't resist machines and projects in this country.

THE PEASANT WOMAN *right:* Alleko Bereshvili, you yourself are the worst one at new projects. That is well known.

THE EXPERT: What about my report? May I write that in your kolchos you will support the transfer of your old valley for the project?

THE PEASANT WOMAN *right:* I will support it. What about you, Alleko?

THE OLD MAN *right, bent over the drawings:* I move that you give us copies of the drawings to take along.

THE PEASANT WOMAN *right:* Then we can sit down to eat. Once he has the drawings and is ready to discuss them, the affair is settled. I know him. And it will be the same with the rest of us.

The delegates embrace again amidst laughter.

THE OLD MAN *left:* Long live the Galinsk kolchos and good luck to your new stud farm!

THE PEASANT WOMAN *left:* Comrades, in honour of the visit of the delegates from the Galinsk kolchos and of the expert we have arranged a play featuring the singer Arkadi Cheidze, which has some bearing on our problem.

Applause.

The girl tractor driver has gone off to fetch the singer.

THE PEASANT WOMAN *right:* Comrades, your play will have to be good. We're going to pay for it with a valley.

THE PEASANT WOMAN *left:* Arkadi Cheidze knows 21,000 verses by heart.

THE OLD MAN *left:* We rehearsed the play under his direction. It is very difficult to get him, by the way. You and the Planning Commission should see to it that he comes north more often, comrade.

THE EXPERT: We are more concerned with economy.

THE OLD MAN *left, smiling:* You arrange the new distribution of grapevines and tractors. Why not of songs, too?

Enter the singer Arkadi Cheidze, led by the girl tractor driver. He is a sturdy man of simple manners, accompanied by musicians with their instruments. The artistes are greeted with applause.

THE GIRL TRACTOR DRIVER: This is the comrade expert, Arkadi.

The singer greets those round him.

THE PEASANT WOMAN *right:* I am very honoured to make your acquaintance. I've heard about your songs ever since I was at school.

THE SINGER: This time it's a play with songs, and almost the whole kolchos takes part. We have brought along the old masks.

THE OLD MAN *right:* Is it going to be one of the old legends?

THE SINGER: A very old one. It is called 'The Chalk Circle' and is derived from the Chinese. But we will recite it in a changed version. Yura, show the masks. Comrades, we consider it an honour to entertain you after such a difficult debate. We hope you will find that the voice of the old poet also sounds well in the shadow of Soviet tractors. It may be mistaken to mix different wines, but old and new wisdom mix very well. Now I hope we will all be given something to eat before the recital begins. That usually helps.

VOICES: Of course.—Everyone into the club house.

All go cheerfully to the meal. While they begin to move off, the expert turns to the singer.

THE EXPERT: How long will the story take, Arkadi? I have to get back to Tiflis tonight.

THE SINGER *casually:* It is actually two stories. A few hours.

THE EXPERT *very confidentially:* Couldn't you make it shorter?

THE SINGER: No.

2

THE NOBLE CHILD

THE SINGER, *who is seen sitting on the floor in front of his musicians, a black sheepskin cloak round his shoulders, leafing through a small, well-thumbed script:*

> Once upon a time
> A time of bloodshed
> When this city was called
> The city of the damned
> It had a Governor.
> His name was Georgi Abashvili
> Once upon a time.
>
> He was very rich
> He had a beautiful wife
> He had a healthy child
> Once upon a time.
>
> No other governor in Grusinia
> Had as many horses in his stable
> As many beggars on his doorstep
> As many soldiers in his service
> As many petitioners in his courtyard
> Once upon a time.
>
> Georgi Abashvili, how shall I describe him?
> He enjoyed his life:
> On Easter Sunday morning
> The Governor and his family went to church
> Once upon a time.

Beggars and petitioners stream from a palace gateway, holding up thin children, crutches, and petitions. They are followed by two Ironshirts and then by the Governor's family, elaborately dressed.

THE BEGGARS AND PETITIONERS: Mercy, Your Grace, the taxes are beyond our means ... I lost my leg in the

Persian War, where can I get . . . My brother is innocent, Your Grace, a misunderstanding . . . My child is starving in my arms . . . We plead for our son's discharge from the army, our one remaining son . . . Please, Your Grace, the water inspector is corrupt.

A servant collects the petitions, another distributes coins from a purse. Soldiers push back the crowd, lashing at it with thick leather whips.

SOLDIER: Get back! Make way at the church door!

Behind the Governor, his wife and his Adjutant, the Governor's child is driven through the gateway in an ornate pram. The crowd surges forward to see it.

THE SINGER *while the crowd is driven back with whips:*

> For the first time on this Easter Sunday, the people see the heir.
>
> Two doctors never leave the child, the noble child
>
> Apple of the Governor's eye.

Cries from the crowd: 'The child!' . . . 'I can't see it, stop pushing!' . . . 'God bless the child, Your Grace!'

THE SINGER:

> Even the mighty Prince Kazbeki
>
> Bows before it at the church door.

A fat prince steps forward and bows before the family.

THE FAT PRINCE: Happy Easter, Natella Abashvili!

A command is heard. A rider arrives at the gallop and holds out to the Governor a roll of documents. At a nod from the Governor the Adjutant, a handsome young man, approaches the rider and stops him. There follows a brief pause during which the fat prince eyes the rider suspiciously.

THE FAT PRINCE: What a magnificent day! While it was raining in the night I thought to myself: gloomy holidays. But this morning: a gay sky. I love a bright sky, a simple heart, Natella Abashvili. And little Michael, a governor from head to foot, tititi! *He tickles the child.* Happy Easter, little Michael, tititi!

THE GOVERNOR'S WIFE: What do you think of this, Arsen? Georgi has finally decided to start building the new wing on the east side. All these miserable slum houses are to be torn down to make room for a garden.

THE FAT PRINCE: That's good news after so much bad. What's the latest about the war, Brother Georgi? *The Governor shows his lack of interest.* A strategic retreat, I hear? Well, minor reverses invariably occur. Sometimes things go well, sometimes not so well. Such are the fortunes of war. Doesn't mean much, eh?

THE GOVERNOR'S WIFE: He's coughing! Georgi, did you hear?
Sharply to the two doctors, dignified men, who stand close to the pram: He's coughing!

FIRST DOCTOR *to the second:* May I remind you, Niko Mikadze, that I was against the lukewarm bath? A minor oversight in warming the bath water, Your Grace.

SECOND DOCTOR *equally polite:* I can't possibly agree with you, Mikha Loladze. The temperature of the bath water was the one prescribed by our great and beloved Mishiko Oboladze. More likely a slight draught in the night, Your Grace.

THE GOVERNOR'S WIFE: But do take better care of him. He looks feverish, Georgi.

FIRST DOCTOR *bending over the child:* No cause for alarm, Your Grace. The bath water will be warmer. It won't happen again.

SECOND DOCTOR *with a poisonous glance at the first:* I won't forget it, dear Mikha Loladze. No cause for alarm, Your Grace.

THE FAT PRINCE: Well, well, well! I always say: one pain in my liver and the doctor gets fifty strokes on the soles of his feet. And that's only because we live in such a decadent age. In the old days it would have been: Off with his head!

THE GOVERNOR'S WIFE: Let's go into the church. Very likely it's the draught here.
The procession, consisting of the family and servants, turns into the church doorway. The fat prince follows. The Adjutant leaves the procession and points at the rider.

THE GOVERNOR: Not before divine service, Shalva.

ADJUTANT *to the rider*: The Governor doesn't want to be
bothered with reports before the service—especially if they
are, as I suspect, of a depressing nature. Go and get yourself
something to eat in the kitchen, my friend.

*The Adjutant joins the procession while the rider enters the palace
gateway, cursing. A soldier appears from the palace and remains
standing in the gateway.*

THE SINGER

> The city lies still.
> On the church square the pigeons preen themselves.
> A soldier of the palace guard
> Is jesting with the kitchen maid
> As she comes up from the river with a bundle.

*A girl tries to pass through the gateway, a bundle of large green
leaves under her arm.*

THE SOLDIER: What! The young lady is not in church?
Shirking service?

GRUSHA: I was already dressed to go. But they wanted one
more goose for the Easter banquet. And they asked me to
fetch it. I know something about geese.

THE SOLDIER: A goose? *Feigning suspicion.* I'd like to see that
goose.

Grusha doesn't understand.

One has to be on one's guard with women. They say: 'I
only went to fetch a goose', and then it turns out to be
something quite different.

GRUSHA *walks resolutely towards him and shows him the goose*:
There it is. And if it isn't a fifteen-pound goose, and they
haven't stuffed it with corn, I'll eat the feathers.

THE SOLDIER: A queen of a goose. It will be eaten by the
Governor himself. So the young lady has been down to the
river again?

GRUSHA: Yes, at the poultry farm.

THE SOLDIER: I see! At the poultry farm, down by the river.
Not higher up, near those—those willows?

GRUSHA: I go to the willows only to wash linen.

THE SOLDIER *insinuatingly:* Exactly.

GRUSHA: Exactly what?

THE SOLDIER *winking:* Exactly that.

GRUSHA: Why shouldn't I wash my linen near the willows?

THE SOLDIER *with exaggerated laughter:* 'Why shouldn't I wash my linen near the willows!' That's a good one, that is!

GRUSHA: I don't understand the soldier. What's so good about it?

THE SOLDIER *slyly:* If someone knew what someone's told, she'd grow hot, she'd grow cold.

GRUSHA: I don't know what I could know about those willows.

THE SOLDIER: Not even if there were a bush opposite? From which everything could be seen? Everything that happens there when a certain person is washing linen?

GRUSHA: What happens there? Won't the soldier say what he means and have done with it?

THE SOLDIER: Something happens. And perhaps something can be seen.

GRUSHA: Could the soldier mean that—once in a while on a hot day—I put my toes in the water? For otherwise there's nothing.

THE SOLDIER: And more—the toes and more.

GRUSHA: More what? At most the foot.

THE SOLDIER: The foot and a little more. *He laughs heartily.*

GRUSHA *angrily:* Simon Chachava, you ought to be ashamed of yourself! To sit in a bush on a hot day and wait till someone comes along and puts her leg in the river! And most likely with another soldier! *She runs off.*

THE SOLDIER *shouting after her:* Not with another soldier!
As the singer resumes his story the soldier runs after Grusha.

THE SINGER

> The city lies still, but why are there armed men?
> The Governor's palace lies at peace
> But why is it a fortress?

From the doorway at the left the fat prince enters quickly. He stands still and looks around. Before the gateway at the right two Ironshirts are waiting. Noticing them, the prince walks slowly past them, signs to them, then exits quickly. One Ironshirt exits through the gateway, the other remains on guard. Muffled voices come from different sides in the rear: 'To your posts!' The palace is surrounded. Distant church bells. Enter through the doorway the procession and the Governor's family returning from church.

THE SINGER

Then the Governor returned to his palace
Then the fortress was a trap
Then the goose was plucked and roasted
Then the goose was no longer eaten
Then noon was no longer the hour to eat
Then noon was the hour to die.

THE GOVERNOR'S WIFE *in passing:* It's quite impossible to live in this slum. But Georgi, of course, builds only for his little Michael. Never for me. Michael is everything, everything for Michael!

THE GOVERNOR: Did you hear Brother Kazbeki bid me a 'Happy Easter'? That's all very well, but so far as I know it didn't rain in Nukha last night. It rained where Brother Kazbeki was. Where was Brother Kazbeki?

THE ADJUTANT: That will have to be investigated.

THE GOVERNOR: Yes, at once. Tomorrow.

The procession turns into the gateway. The rider, who has meanwhile returned from the palace, walks towards the Governor.

THE ADJUTANT: Don't you want to listen to the rider from the capital, Your Excellency? He arrived this morning with confidential papers.

THE GOVERNOR *in passing:* Not before the banquet, Shalva!

THE ADJUTANT *to the rider, while the procession disappears into the palace and only two Ironshirts remain at the gate as palace guards:* The Governor doesn't wish to be disturbed by military reports before the banquet. The afternoon His Excellency will devote to conferences with prominent architects who have also been invited to the banquet. Here they are already. *Enter three men. As the rider goes off, the Adjutant greets the architects.* Gentlemen, His Excellency is awaiting you at the banquet. His entire time will be devoted to you. To the great new plans! Come, let us go!

ONE OF THE ARCHITECTS: We are impressed that his Excellency thinks of building in spite of the disquieting rumours that the war in Persia has taken a turn for the worse.

THE ADJUTANT: All the more reason for building! That's nothing. Persia is far away. The garrison here would let itself be chopped to pieces for its Governor.

Uproar from the palace. Shrill screams of a woman. Orders are shouted. Dumbfounded, the Adjutant moves towards the gateway. An Ironshirt steps out and holds him up at the point of a lance.

What's going on here? Put down that lance, you dog! *To the palace guard, furiously.* Disarm him! Can't you see an attempt is being made on the Governor's life?

The palace guard Ironshirts refuse to obey. Staring coldly, indifferently, at the Adjutant, they watch the proceedings without interest. The Adjutant fights his way into the palace.

ONE OF THE ARCHITECTS: The Princes! Don't you realize that the Princes met last night in the capital? And that they are against the Grand Duke and his governors? Gentlemen, we'd better make ourselves scarce.

They rush off.

THE SINGER

Oh, blindness of the great! They walk like gods
Great over bent backs, sure
Of hired fists, trusting
In their power which has already lasted so long.
But long is not forever.
Oh, Wheel of Fortune! Hope of the people!

From the gateway, enter the Governor with a grey face, manacled, between two soldiers armed to the teeth.

Walk, Your Highness, walk even now with head up.
From your Palace the eyes of many foes follow you!
You no longer need an architect, a carpenter will do.

You will not move into a new palace, but into a little hole
in the ground.

Just look about you once more, you blind man!

The arrested Governor looks about him.

Does all you once possessed still please you? Between the
Easter Mass and the banquet

You are walking to that place from which no one returns.

*The Governor is led away. The palace guard follows. A horn
sounds. Noise behind the gateway.*

When the houses of the great collapse

Many little people are slain.

Those who had no share in the fortunes of the mighty

Often have a share in their misfortunes. The plunging
wain

Drags the sweating beasts with it into the abyss.

Servants come rushing through the gateway in panic.

THE SERVANTS *in confusion:* The hampers!—Take them all
into the third courtyard! Food for five days!—Her Ladyship has fainted! Someone must carry her down. She must
get away.—And what about us? We'll be slaughtered like
chickens, it's the old story.—Jesus and Mary, what's going
to happen? There's already bloodshed in the town, they
say.—Nonsense, the Governor has just been asked politely
to appear at a Princes' meeting. Everything'll be all right. I
have this on the best authority.

The two doctors rush into the courtyard.

FIRST DOCTOR *trying to restrain the other:* Niko Mikadze, it is
your duty as a doctor to attend Natella Abashvili.

SECOND DOCTOR: My duty? It's yours!

FIRST DOCTOR: Niko Mikadze, who is in charge of the child
today? You or me?

SECOND DOCTOR: Do you really think, Mikha Loladze, I'm
going to stay another minute in this cursed house for that
little brat?

*They start fighting. All one hears is: 'You neglect your duty!' and
'Duty be damned!' Then the second doctor knocks down the first.*

SECOND DOCTOR: Oh, go to hell! *Exit.*

THE SERVANTS: There's time enough before night. The soldiers won't be drunk till then.—Does anyone know if they've started a mutiny yet?—The Palace Guard has ridden away.—Doesn't anyone know what's happened?

GRUSHA: Meliva the fisherman says a comet with a red tail has been seen in the sky over the capital. That means bad luck.

THE SERVANTS: Yesterday they were saying in the capital that the Persian War is lost.—The Princes have started a great revolt. There's a rumour that the Grand Duke has already fled. All his Governors are to be hanged.—The likes of us will be left alone. I have a brother in the Ironshirts.

Enter the soldier Simon Chachava, searching the crowd for Grusha.

THE ADJUTANT *appearing in the doorway:* Everyone into the third courtyard! All hands help with the packing!

He drives the servants out. Simon finally finds Grusha.

SIMON: There you are at last, Grusha! What are you going to do?

GRUSHA: Nothing. If the worst comes to the worst, I've a brother with a farm in the mountains. But what about you?

SIMON: Don't worry about me. *Polite again.* Grusha Vachnadze, your desire to know my plans fills me with satisfaction. I've been ordered to accompany Madam Natella Abashvili as her guard.

GRUSHA: But hasn't the Palace Guard mutinied?

SIMON *serious:* That they have.

GRUSHA: But isn't it dangerous to accompany the woman?

SIMON: In Tiflis they say: how can stabbing harm the knife?

GRUSHA: You're not a knife. You're a man, Simon Chachava. What has this woman to do with you?

SIMON: The woman has nothing to do with me. But I have my orders, and so I go.

GRUSHA: The soldier is a pig-headed man; he gets himself into danger for nothing—nothing at all. *As she is called from the palace:* Now I must go into the third courtyard. I'm in a hurry.

SIMON: As there's a hurry we oughtn't to quarrel. For a good quarrel one needs time. May I ask if the young lady still has parents?

GRUSHA: No, only a brother.

SIMON: As time is short—the second question would be: Is the young lady as healthy as a fish in water?

GRUSHA: Perhaps once in a while a pain in the right shoulder; but otherwise strong enough for any work. So far no one has complained.

SIMON: Everyone knows that. Even if it's Easter Sunday and there's the question who shall fetch the goose, then it's she. The third question is this: Is the young lady impatient? Does she want cherries in winter?

GRUSHA: Impatient, no. But if a man goes to war without any reason, and no message comes, that's bad.

SIMON: A message will come. *Grusha is again called from the palace.* And finally the main question . . .

GRUSHA: Simon Chachava, because I've got to go to the third courtyard and I'm in a hurry, the answer is 'Yes'.

SIMON *very embarrassed:* Hurry, they say, is the wind that blows down the scaffolding. But they also say: The rich don't know what hurry is.—I come from . . .

GRUSHA: Kutsk.

SIMON: So the young lady has already made inquiries? Am healthy, have no dependents, earn ten piastres a month, as a paymaster twenty, and am asking honourably for your hand.

GRUSHA: Simon Chachava, that suits me.

SIMON *taking from his neck a thin chain from which hangs a little cross:* This cross belonged to my mother, Grusha Vachnadze. The chain is silver. Please wear it.

GRUSHA: I thank you, Simon. *He fastens it round her neck.*

SIMON: Now I must harness the horses. The young lady will understand that. It would be better for the young lady to go into the third courtyard. Otherwise there'll be trouble.

GRUSHA: Yes, Simon.

They stand together undecided.

SIMON: I'll just take the woman to the troops who've remained loyal. When the war's over, I'll come back. In two
weeks. Or three. I hope my intended won't get tired waiting
for my return.

GRUSHA: Simon Chachava, I shall wait for you.

> Go calmly into battle, soldier
> The bloody battle, the bitter battle
> From which not everyone returns.
> When you return I will be there.
> I will be waiting for you under the green elm
> I will be waiting for you under the bare elm
> I will wait until the last soldier has returned
> And even longer.
> When you return from the battle
> No boots will lie before the door
> The pillow beside mine will be empty
> My mouth will be unkissed.
> When you return, when you return
> You will be able to say: all is as it was.

SIMON: I thank you, Grusha Vachnadze, and farewell!
*He bows low before her; she bows low before him. Then she runs off
without looking round. Enter the Adjutant from the gateway.*

THE ADJUTANT *harshly:* Harness the horses to the big
carriage! Don't stand there doing nothing, idiot!
*Simon Chachava leaps to attention and goes off. Two servants crawl
in from the gateway, loaded down with heavy trunks. Behind them,
supported by her women, stumbles Natella Abashvili. She is
followed by another woman carrying Michael.*

THE GOVERNOR'S WIFE: As usual, nobody's paying the
slightest attention. I hardly know if I'm standing on my
head or my feet. Where's Michael? Don't hold him so
clumsily! Pile the trunks on to the carriage! Shalva, is there
any word from the Governor?

THE ADJUTANT *shaking his head:* You must get away at once.

THE GOVERNOR'S WIFE: Is there any news from the town?

THE ADJUTANT: No. So far all is quiet. But there isn't a minute to lose. There's not enough room for the trunks on the carriage. Please pick out what you need.
Exit the Adjutant quickly.

THE GOVERNOR'S WIFE: Only essentials! Quick, open the trunks. I'll tell you what I've got to have.
The trunks are lowered and opened.

THE GOVERNOR'S WIFE *pointing at some brocade dresses:* That green one! And of course that one with the fur trimming. Where are the doctors? I'm getting this terrible migraine again. It always starts in the temples. This one with the little pearl buttons . . . *Enter Grusha.* You're taking your time, eh? Go and get the hot water bottles at once!
Grusha runs off, and returns with hot water bottles. The Governor's wife orders her about by signs.

THE GOVERNOR'S WIFE *watching a young woman attendant:* Don't tear the sleeve!

THE YOUNG WOMAN: I promise you, madam, no harm has come to the dress.

THE GOVERNOR'S WIFE: Because I caught you. I've been watching you for a long time. Nothing in your head but making eyes at the Adjutant. I'll kill you, you bitch! *She beats her.*

THE ADJUTANT *returning:* I must ask you to make haste, Natella Abashvili. They are fighting in the town. *Exit the Adjutant.*

THE GOVERNOR'S WIFE *letting go of the young woman:* My God, do you think they'll do something to me? Why should they? *All are silent. She herself begins to rummage in the trunks.* Where's my brocade jacket? Help me! What about Michael? Is he asleep?

THE NURSE: Yes, madam.

THE GOVERNOR'S WIFE: Then put him down a moment and go and fetch my little morocco slippers from the bedchamber. I need them to go with the green dress. *The nurse puts down the child and goes off. To the young woman:* Don't stand around, you! *The young woman runs off.* Stay here, or I'll have you flogged! Just look at the way these things have been packed! No love! No understanding! If one doesn't give every order oneself . . . At such moments one realizes what one's servants are like! Masha! *She gives her an order with a wave of the hand.* You all gorge yourselves, but never a sign of gratitude! I won't forget this.

THE ADJUTANT *very excited:* Natella, you must leave at once! Orbeliani, Judge of the Supreme Court, has just been hanged! The carpet weavers are in revolt!

THE GOVERNOR'S WIFE: Why? I must have the silver dress —it cost 1000 piastres. And that one there, and all my furs. And where's the wine-coloured dress?

THE ADJUTANT *trying to pull her away:* Riots have broken out in the outer town! We've got to leave this minute! *A servant runs off.* Where's the child?

THE GOVERNOR'S WIFE *to the nurse:* Maro, get the child ready! Where are you?

THE ADJUTANT *leaving:* We'll probably have to do without the carriage. And ride.

The Governor's wife still rummages among her dresses, throws some on to the heap to go with her, then takes them off again. Drums are heard. The sky begins to redden.

THE GOVERNOR'S WIFE *rummaging desperately:* I can't find that wine-coloured dress. *Shrugging her shoulders, to the second woman:* Take the whole heap and carry it to the carriage. Why hasn't Maro come back? Have you all gone off your heads? I told you it's right at the bottom.

THE ADJUTANT *returning:* Quick! Quick!

THE GOVERNOR'S WIFE *to the second woman:* Run! Just throw them into the carriage!

THE ADJUTANT: We're not going by carriage. Come at once or I'll ride off on my own!

THE GOVERNOR'S WIFE: Maro! Bring the child! *To the second woman:* Go and look, Masha. No, first take the dresses to the carriage. It's all nonsense, I wouldn't dream of riding! *Turning round, she sees the fire-reddened sky and starts back in horror.* Fire! *She rushes off, followed by the Adjutant. The second woman, shaking her head, follows with a heap of dresses. Servants enter from the gateway.*

THE COOK: That must be the East Gate that's burning.

THE CHEF: They've gone. And without the food wagon. How are we going to get away now?

A STABLEMAN: This is going to be an unhealthy place for some time. *To the third chambermaid:* Suleika, I'm going to fetch some blankets, we're clearing out.

THE NURSE *entering through the gateway with her mistress's slippers:* Madam!

A FAT WOMAN: She's gone.

THE NURSE: And the child. *She rushes to the child, and picks it up.* They left it behind, those brutes! *She hands the child to Grusha.* Hold it for a moment. *Deceitfully.* I'm going to look for the carriage.

She runs off, following the Governor's wife.

GRUSHA: What have they done to the Governor?

THE STABLEMAN *drawing his index finger across his throat:* Fft.

THE FAT WOMAN *seeing the gesture, becomes hysterical:* Oh God! Oh God! Oh God! Our master Georgi Abashvili! At morning Mass he was a picture of health! And now! Oh, take me away! We're all lost! We must die in sin! Like our master, Georgi Abashvili!

THE THIRD WOMAN *trying to calm her:* Calm down, Nina. You'll get away. You've done no one any harm.

THE FAT WOMAN *being led out:* Oh God! Oh God! Oh God! Let's all get out before they come! Before they come!

THE THIRD WOMAN: Nina takes it to heart more than the mistress. People like that get others even to do their weeping for them! *Seeing the child in Grusha's arms.* The child! What are you doing with it?

GRUSHA: It's been left behind.

THE THIRD WOMAN: She just left it? Michael, who was never allowed to be in a draught!

The servants gather round the child.

GRUSHA: He's waking up.

THE STABLEMAN: Better put him down, I tell you. I'd rather not think what'd happen to the person seen with that child. I'll get our things. You wait here. *Exit into the palace.*

THE COOK: He's right. Once they start they slaughter whole families. I'll go and fetch my belongings.

All go except the cook, the third woman and Grusha with the child in her arms.

THE THIRD WOMAN: Didn't you hear? Better put him down!

GRUSHA: The nurse asked me to hold him for a moment.

THE COOK: That one won't come back, you silly!

THE THIRD WOMAN: Keep your hands off him.

THE COOK: They'll be more after him than after his mother. He's the heir. Grusha, you're a good soul. But you know you're not too bright. I tell you, if he had the plague it couldn't be worse. Better see to it that you get away.

The stableman has come back carrying bundles which he distributes among the women. All except Grusha prepare to leave.

GRUSHA *stubbornly:* He hasn't got the plague. He looks at you like a human being.

THE COOK: Then don't you look back. You're just the kind of fool who always gets put upon. If someone says to you: Run and get the lettuce, you have the longest legs!—you run. We're taking the ox-cart, you can have a lift if you hurry. Jesus, by now the whole neighbourhood must be in flames!

THE THIRD WOMAN: Haven't you packed anything yet? There isn't much time, you know. The Ironshirts will soon be here from the barracks.

Exit both women and the stableman.

GRUSHA: I'm coming.

Grusha lays the child down, looks at it for a moment, then takes clothes from the trunks lying about and covers the sleeping child. Then she runs into the palace to get her things. Sounds of horses' hoofs and of women screaming. Enter the fat prince with drunken Ironshirts. One of them carries the head of the Governor on a lance.

THE FAT PRINCE: Put it here. Right in the middle! *One Iron-shirt climbs on to the back of another, takes the head and holds it over the gateway.* That's not the middle. Further to the right. Good. What I do, my friends, I do well. *While an Ironshirt with hammer and nail fastens the head by its hair:* This morning at the church door I said to Georgi Abashvili: 'I love a clear sky'. Actually, what I prefer is lightning from a clear sky. Oh, yes. But it's a pity they took the brat away. I need him. Badly. Search the whole of Grusinia for him! 1000 piastres reward!

As Grusha enters cautiously through the doorway, the fat prince and the Ironshirts leave. Trampling of horses' hoofs again. Carrying a bundle, Grusha walks towards the gateway. At the last moment, she turns to see if the child is still there. Promptly the singer begins to sing. She stands rooted to the spot.

THE SINGER

As she was standing between courtyard and gate, she
    heard
Or thought she heard, a low voice. The child
Called to her, not whining but calling quite sensibly
At least so it seemed to her: 'Woman', it said, 'Help me'.
Went on calling not whining but calling quite sensibly:
'Don't you know, woman, that she who does not listen to
    a cry for help
But passes by shutting her ears, will never hear
The gentle call of a lover
Nor the blackbird at dawn, nor the happy
Sigh of the exhausted grape-picker at the sound of the
    Angelus.'
Hearing this

Grusha walks a few steps towards the child and bends over it.

                    she went back to the child
Just for one more look, just to sit with it
For a moment or two till someone should come
Its mother, perhaps, or someone else—

She sits down opposite the child, and leans against a trunk.

Just for a moment before she left, for now the danger was
    too great
The city full of flame and grief.

The light grows dimmer as though evening and night were falling,
Grusha has gone into the palace and fetched a lamp and some milk,
which she gives the child to drink.

THE SINGER *loudly:*

Terrible is the temptation to do good!

Grusha now settles down to keep watch over the child through the
night. Once, she lights a small lamp to look at it. Once, she tucks it
in with a brocade coat. Now and again she listens and looks up to
see if someone is coming.

For a long time she sat with the child.
Evening came, night came, dawn came.
Too long she sat, too long she watched
The soft breathing, the little fists
Till towards morning the temptation grew too strong.
She rose, she leaned over, she sighed, she lifted the child
She carried it off.

She does what the singer says as he describes it.

Like booty she took it for herself
Like a thief she sneaked away.

3

THE FLIGHT INTO THE NORTHERN MOUNTAINS

THE SINGER

As Grusha Vachnadze left the city
On the Grusinian highway
Towards the northern mountains
She sang a song, she bought some milk.

THE MUSICIANS

How will the merciful escape the merciless
The bloodhounds, the trappers?
Into the deserted mountains she wandered
Along the Grusinian highway she wandered
She sang a song, she bought some milk.

Grusha Vachnadze continues on her way. On her back she carries
the child in a sack, in one hand a bundle, in the other a big stick.

GRUSHA *singing:*

> Four generals set off for Iran
> Four generals but not one man.
> The first did not strike a blow
> The second did not beat the foe
> For the third the weather was not right
> For the fourth the soldiers would not fight.
> Four generals went forth to attack
> Four generals turned back.

> Sosso Robakidse marched to Iran
> Sosso Robakidse was a man.
> He struck a sturdy blow
> He certainly beat the foe
> For him the weather was good enough
> For him the soldiers fought with love
> Sosso Robakidse marched to Iran
> Sosso Robakidse is our man.

A peasant's cottage appears.

GRUSHA *to the child:* Noontime, eating time. Now we'll sit here quietly in the grass, while the good Grusha goes and buys a little jug of milk. *She lays the child down and knocks at the cottage door. An old peasant opens it.* Grandpa, could I have a little mug of milk? And perhaps a corn cake?

THE OLD MAN: Milk? We haven't any milk. The soldiers from the city took our goats. If you want milk, go to the soldiers.

GRUSHA: But Grandpa, you surely have a jug of milk for a child?

THE OLD MAN: And for a 'God Bless You', eh?

GRUSHA: Who said anything about a 'God Bless You'? *She pulls out her purse.* We're going to pay like princes. Head in the clouds, bottom in the water! *The peasant goes off grumbling to fetch milk.* And how much is this jug?

THE OLD MAN: Three piastres. Milk has gone up.

GRUSHA: Three piastres for that drop? *Without a word the old man slams the door in her face.* Michael, did you hear that?

Three piastres! We can't afford that. *She goes back, sits down again and gives the child her breast.* Well, we must try again like this. Suck. Think of the three piastres. There's nothing there, but you think you're drinking, and that's something. *Shaking her head, she realizes the child has stopped sucking. She gets up, walks back to the door, and knocks again.* Open, Grandpa, we'll pay. *Under her breath:* May God strike you! *When the old man appears again:* I thought it would be half a piastre. But the child must have something. What about one piastre?

THE OLD MAN: Two.

GRUSHA: Don't slam the door again. *She rummages a long time in her purse.* Here are two piastres. But this milk has got to last. We still have a long journey ahead of us. These are cut-throat prices. It's a sin.

THE OLD MAN: If you want milk, kill the soldiers.

GRUSHA *letting the child drink:* That's an expensive joke. Drink, Michael. This is half a week's pay. The people here think we've earned our money sitting on our bottom. Michael, Michael, I certainly took on a nice burden with you! *Looking at the brocade coat in which the child is wrapped:* A brocade coat worth 1000 piastres, and not one piastre for milk. *She glances round.* Look! There's a carriage, with rich ladies. We ought to get on to that.

In front of a caravansary. Grusha dressed in the brocade coat is seen approaching two elegant ladies. She holds the child in her arms.

GRUSHA: Oh, you ladies want to spend the night here, too? It's awful how crowded it is everywhere! And not a carriage to be found! My coachman simply turned back. I've been walking half a mile on foot. Barefoot, too! My Persian shoes—you know those heels! But why doesn't someone come?

THE ELDER LADY: That innkeeper certainly takes his time. The whole country has lost its manners since those goings-on started in the capital.

The innkeeper appears, a very dignified old man with a long beard, followed by his servant.

THE INNKEEPER: Excuse an old man for keeping you waiting, ladies. My little grandchild was showing me a peach tree in blossom. There on the slope, beyond the cornfields. We're planting fruit trees there, a few cherries. Further west—*pointing*—the ground gets more stony. That's where the farmers graze their sheep. You ought to see the peach blossom, the pink is exquisite.

THE ELDER LADY: You live in a fertile region.

THE INNKEEPER: God has blessed it. How far on is the fruit-blossom further south, my ladies? I take it you come from the south?

THE YOUNGER LADY: I must admit I haven't been paying much attention to the landscape.

THE INNKEEPER *politely:* Of course, the dust. It is advisable to travel slowly on our high roads. Provided, of course, one isn't in too great a hurry.

THE ELDER LADY: Put your scarf round your throat, dearest. The evening breeze seems rather cool here.

THE INNKEEPER: It comes down from the Janga-Tau glaciers, my ladies.

GRUSHA: Yes, I'm afraid my son may catch cold.

THE ELDER LADY: A very spacious caravansary! Shall we go in?

THE INNKEEPER: Oh, the ladies want rooms? But the caravansary is full up, my ladies. And the servants have run off. I very much regret it, but I cannot accommodate another person, not even with references . . .

THE YOUNGER LADY: But we can't spend the night here on the road.

THE ELDER LADY *drily:* How much?

THE INNKEEPER: My ladies, you will understand that in these times, when so many fugitives, no doubt quite respectable people but not popular with the authorities, are looking for shelter, a house has to be particularly careful. Therefore . . .

THE ELDER LADY: My dear man, we aren't fugitives. We're simply moving to our summer residence in the mountains,

that's all. It would never occur to us to ask for hospitality
if—we needed it all that urgently.

THE INNKEEPER *nodding his head in agreement:* Of course not.
I only doubt if the tiny room at my disposal would suit the
ladies. I have to charge 60 piastres per person. Are the ladies
together?

GRUSHA: In a way. I'm also in need of shelter.

THE YOUNGER LADY: 60 piastres! That's a cut-throat
price.

THE INNKEEPER *coldly:* My ladies, I have no desire to cut
throats. That's why . . . *He turns to go.*

THE ELDER LADY: Must we talk about throats? Let's go in.
She enters, followed by the servant.

THE YOUNGER LADY *desperate:* 180 piastres for one room!
Glancing back at Grusha: But with the child it's impossible!
What if it cries?

THE INNKEEPER: The room costs 180, whether it's two
persons or three.

THE YOUNGER LADY *changing her attitude to Grusha:* On the
other hand, I couldn't bear to think of you on the road, my
dear. Do come in.
*They enter the caravansary. From the rear on the opposite side of
the stage the servant appears with some luggage. Behind him come
the elder lady, the younger lady and Grusha with the child.*

THE YOUNGER LADY: 180 piastres! I haven't been so upset
since they brought dear Igor home.

THE ELDER LADY: Must you talk about Igor?

THE YOUNGER LADY: Actually, we are four persons. The
child is one too, isn't it? *To Grusha:* Couldn't you pay half
at least?

GRUSHA: That's impossible. I had to leave in a hurry, you see.
And the Adjutant forgot to slip me enough money.

THE ELDER LADY: Perhaps you haven't even got the 60?

GRUSHA: That much I'll pay.

THE YOUNGER LADY: Where are the beds?

THE SERVANT: There aren't any beds. Here are some sacks
and blankets. You'll have to arrange them yourselves. Be

glad you're not being put in a hole in the earth. Like lots of others. *Exit*.

THE YOUNGER LADY: Did you hear that? I'm going straight to the innkeeper. That man must be flogged.

THE ELDER LADY: Like your husband?

THE YOUNGER LADY: Don't be so cruel! *She weeps.*

THE ELDER LADY: How are we going to arrange something to sleep on?

GRUSHA: I'll see to that. *She puts down the child.* It's always easier when there are several hands. You still have the carriage. *Sweeping the floor.* I was taken completely by surprise. 'My dear Anastasia Katarinovska,' my husband was saying before luncheon, 'do go and lie down for a while. You know how easily you get your migraine.' *She spreads out sacks and makes beds. The ladies, watching her work, exchange glances.* 'Georgi', said I to the Governor, 'I can't lie down when there are sixty for luncheon. And one can't trust the servants. And Michael Georgivich won't eat without me.' *To Michael*: See, Michael? Everything'll be all right, what did I tell you! *She suddenly realizes that the ladies are watching her strangely and whispering.* Well, there we are! At least one doesn't have to lie on the bare floor. I've folded the blankets double.

THE ELDER LADY *imperiously*: You seem to be rather clever at making beds, my dear. Let's have a look at your hands!

GRUSHA *frightened*: What?

THE YOUNGER LADY: You're being asked to show your hands.

Grusha shows the ladies her hands.

THE YOUNGER LADY *triumphant*: Cracked! A servant!

THE ELDER LADY *goes to the door and shouts*: Service!

THE YOUNGER LADY: You're caught! You swindler! Just confess what mischief you're up to!

GRUSHA *confused*: I'm not up to any mischief. I just thought you might take us a little way in your carriage. Please, I ask you, don't make a noise, I'll go on my own.

THE YOUNGER LADY *while the elder lady continues shouting for service:* Yes, you'll go all right, but with the police. For the moment you'll stay. Don't you dare move, you!

GRUSHA: But I was ready to pay the 60 piastres. Here. *She shows her purse.* Look for yourself. I have them. Here are four tens, and here's a five—no, that's another ten, and ten, makes 60. All I want is to get the child on to the carriage. That's the truth.

THE YOUNGER LADY: Aha, so that's what you want. On to the carriage! Now it's come out.

GRUSHA: Madam, I confess, I am from a humble family. Please don't call the police. The child is of noble birth, look at the linen. It's fleeing, like yourself.

THE YOUNGER LADY: Of noble birth! We know that one. The father's a prince, eh?

GRUSHA *to the elder lady, fiercely:* Stop shouting! Have you no heart at all?

THE YOUNGER LADY *to the elder lady:* Look out! She'll attack you! She's dangerous! Help! Murder!

THE SERVANT *entering:* What's going on here?

THE ELDER LADY: This person here has smuggled herself in by playing the lady. She's probably a thief.

THE YOUNGER LADY: And a dangerous one, too. She wanted to murder us. It's a case for the police. Oh God, I can feel my migraine coming on!

THE SERVANT: There aren't any police at the moment. *To Grusha:* Pack up your things, sister, and make yourself scarce.

GRUSHA *angrily picking up the child:* You monsters! And they're already nailing your heads to the wall!

THE SERVANT *pushing her out:* Shut your trap. Or you'll have the Old Man here. And there's no trifling with him.

THE ELDER LADY *to the younger lady:* Just see if she hasn't stolen something already!

While the ladies, right, look feverishly to see whether something has been stolen, the servant and Grusha go out through the door, left.

THE SERVANT: Look before you leap, I say. Another time have a good look at people before you get mixed up with them.

GRUSHA: I thought they'd be more likely to treat their own kind better.

THE SERVANT: Not them! Believe me, nothing's harder than aping a lazy useless person. Once they suspect you can wipe your own arse, or that your hands have ever touched a broom, the game's up. Just wait a minute, I'll get you a corn cake and a few apples.

GRUSHA: Better not. I must get out before the Old Man comes. And if I walk all night I'll be out of danger, I think. *She walks away.*

THE SERVANT *calling after her in a low voice:* At the next crossroads, turn right.
She disappears.

THE SINGER:

As Grusha Vachnadze wandered northwards
She was followed by the Prince's Ironshirts.

THE MUSICIANS

How will the barefooted girl escape the Ironshirts
The bloodhounds, the trappers?
They are hunting even by night.
Pursuers don't get tired.
Butchers sleep little.

Two Ironshirts are trudging along the highway.

THE CORPORAL: Blockhead, you'll never amount to anything. Why? Because your heart's not in it. Your superior sees it in little things. Yesterday when I laid that fat woman, I admit you collared her husband as I commanded. And you did kick him in the stomach. But did you enjoy it like a good soldier? Or did you just do it from a sense of duty? I've kept my eyes on you, blockhead. You're like a hollow reed or a tinkling cymbal. You'll never get promoted. *They walk awhile in silence.* Don't you get the idea I don't notice how insubordinate you are in every way. I forbid you to limp! You do it simply because I sold the horses, and I

sold them because I'd never have got that price again.
I know you: you limp just to show me you don't like
marching. But that won't help you. It'll go against you.
Sing!

THE TWO IRONSHIRTS *singing:*

O sadly one morning, one morning in May
I kissed my darling and rode far away.
Protect her, dear friends, until home from the wars
I come riding in triumph, alive on my horse.

THE CORPORAL: Louder!

THE TWO IRONSHIRTS:

When I lie in my grave and my sword turns to rust
My darling shall bring me a handful of dust.
For the feet that so gaily ran up to her door
And the arms that went round her shall please her no
more.

They begin to walk again in silence.

THE CORPORAL: A good soldier has his heart and soul in it.
He lets himself be hacked to pieces by his superiors, and
even while dying he's aware of his Corporal nodding ap-
proval. For him that's reward enough. That's all he wants.
But *you* won't get a nod. And you'll croak just the same.
Christ, how am I to lay my hands on the Governor's
bastard with an ass like you!

They trudge on.

THE SINGER

When Grusha Vachnadze came to the River Sirra
The flight grew too much for her, the helpless child too
heavy.

THE MUSICIANS

The rosy dawn in the cornfields
Is nothing but cold to the sleepless.
The gay clatter of the milk cans in the farmyard
Where the smoke rises is nothing but a threat to the
fugitives.
She who drags the child feels nothing but its weight.

Grusha stops in front of a farm.

GRUSHA: Now you've wetted yourself again, and you know I've no nappies. Michael, we've got to part. This is far enough from the city. They won't want you so badly, little squit, that they'll follow you all this way. The woman looks kind, and just you smell the milk! So farewell, little Michael. I'll forget how you kicked me in the back all night to make me go faster. And you—you forget the meagre fare. It was meant well. I'd love to have kept you, because your nose is so small, but it can't be done. I'd have shown you your first rabbit and—how not to wet yourself, but I must turn back, because my sweetheart the soldier might soon return, and suppose he didn't find me? You can't ask that of me, Michael.

A fat peasant woman carries a milk can to the door. Grusha waits until she has gone in, then gingerly approaches the house. She tiptoes to the door and lays the child on the threshold. Then, hiding behind a tree, she waits until the peasant woman opens the door and sees the bundle.

THE PEASANT WOMAN: Jesus Christ, what's this? Husband!

THE PEASANT: What's up? Let me have my soup.

THE PEASANT WOMAN *to the child:* Where's your mother? Haven't you got one? It's a boy. And the linen is fine; it's from a good family. And they just leave him on our doorstep. Oh, what times we live in!

THE PEASANT: If they think we're going to feed it, they're mistaken. You take it to the priest in the village. That's all we can do.

THE PEASANT WOMAN: What will the priest do with it? It needs a mother. There, it's waking up. Don't you think we could keep it?

THE PEASANT *shouting:* No!

THE PEASANT WOMAN: I could lay it in the corner, next to the armchair. I only need a crib for it. And I can take it into the fields with me. Look how it's smiling! Husband, we have a roof over our heads and we can do it. I won't hear another word.

She carries the child into the house. The peasant follows, protesting.

Grusha steps out from behind the tree, laughs, and hurries away in the opposite direction.

THE SINGER

Why so gay, you, making for home?

THE MUSICIANS

Because with a smile the child

Has won new parents for himself, that's why I'm gay.

Because I am rid of the loved one

That's why I'm happy.

THE SINGER

And why are you sad?

THE MUSICIANS

I'm sad because I'm single and free

Of the little burden in whom a heart was beating:

Like one robbed, like one impoverished I'm going.

Grusha walks for a short while, then meets the two Ironshirts, who hold her up at the point of a lance.

THE CORPORAL: Young lady, you're running into the Armed Forces. Where are you coming from? When are you coming? Are you entertaining illegal relations with the enemy? Where is he hiding? What sort of movements is he making in your rear? What about the hills? What about the valley? How are your stockings fastened?

Grusha stands there frightened.

GRUSHA: They are strongly fastened; you'd better withdraw.

THE CORPORAL: I always withdraw. In that respect I'm reliable. Why are you staring like that at the lance? In the field a soldier never loses control of his lance. That's an order. Learn it by heart, blockhead. Now then, young lady, where are you off to?

GRUSHA: To my intended, one Simon Chachava, of the Palace Guard in Nukha. Wait till I write to him; he'll break your bones for you.

THE CORPORAL: Simon Chachava? Indeed! I know him. He gave me the key so I could keep an eye on you once in a while. Blockhead, we're getting unpopular. We must make her realize we have honourable intentions. Young lady, my apparent flippancy hides a serious nature. So I'll tell you officially: I want a child from you.

Grusha utters a little scream.

Blockhead, she has understood. Ooh, isn't that a sweet fright! 'But first I must take the bread out of the oven, Officer! But first I must change my torn chemise, Colonel!' But joking apart. Listen, young lady, we are looking for a certain child in these parts. Have you heard of a child from the city, of good family, dressed in fine linen?

GRUSHA: No. I've heard nothing.

THE SINGER

Run, kind heart! The killers are coming!

Help the helpless child, helpless girl! And so she runs.

Suddenly, panic-stricken, she turns round and runs. The Ironshirts glance at each other, then follow her, cursing.

THE MUSICIANS

In the bloodiest times

There are still good people.

As Grusha enters the cottage, the peasant woman is bending over the child's crib.

GRUSHA: Hide it! Quick! The Ironshirts are coming! It was I who laid it on your doorstep. But it isn't mine. It's of a noble family.

THE PEASANT WOMAN: Who's coming? What sort of Ironshirts?

GRUSHA: Don't ask questions. The Ironshirts who are looking for it.

THE PEASANT WOMAN: They've no business in my house. But it seems I must have a word with you.

GRUSHA: Take off the fine linen. That will give us away.

THE PEASANT WOMAN: Oh, you and your linen! In this house *I* decide. And don't you mess up my room. But why did you abandon it? That's a sin.

GRUSHA *looking out of the window:* There, they're coming from behind the trees. I shouldn't have run away. That gave them ideas. What on earth shall I do?

THE PEASANT WOMAN *looking out of the window and suddenly starting with fear:* Jesus and Mary! Ironshirts!

GRUSHA: They're after the child!

THE PEASANT WOMAN: But suppose they come in!

GRUSHA: You mustn't give it to them. Say it's yours.

THE PEASANT WOMAN: Yes.

GRUSHA: They'll run it through if you let them have it.

THE PEASANT WOMAN: But suppose they demand it? The money for the harvest is in the house.

GRUSHA: If you let them have it, they'll run it through, here in your room! You've got to say it's yours.

THE PEASANT WOMAN: Yes, but suppose they don't believe me?

GRUSHA: You must speak firmly.

THE PEASANT WOMAN: They'll burn the roof over our head.

GRUSHA: That's why you've got to say it's yours. His name's Michael. I shouldn't have told you that.
The peasant woman nods.
Don't nod your head like that. And don't tremble; they'll notice.

THE PEASANT WOMAN: Yes.

GRUSHA: Stop saying yes. I can't stand it any longer. *She shakes her.* Haven't *you* got a child?

THE PEASANT WOMAN *muttering:* In the war.

GRUSHA: Then perhaps he's an Ironshirt, too, by now? And what if he ran children through? You'd give him a fine piece of your mind! 'Stop waving that lance in my room! Is that what I've reared you for? Go and wash your neck before you speak to your mother.'

THE PEASANT WOMAN: That's true, I wouldn't let him behave like that.

GRUSHA: Promise me you'll say it's yours.

THE PEASANT WOMAN: Yes

GRUSHA: There! They're coming!
There is a knocking at the door. The women don't answer. Enter the Ironshirts. The peasant woman bows deeply.

THE CORPORAL: Well, there she is. What did I tell you? My nose. I smelled her. Young lady, I have a question to ask you: Why did you run away? What did you think I would do to you? I'll bet it was something lewd. Confess!

GRUSHA *while the peasant woman continues to bow:* I'd left the milk on the stove. Then I suddenly remembered it.

THE CORPORAL: I thought it was because you imagined I'd looked at you in a lewd way—as if I were thinking there could be something between us. A lustful glance, know what I mean?

GRUSHA: I didn't see that.

THE CORPORAL: But it could have been, eh? You must admit that. After all, I could be a swine. I'm quite frank with you: I could think of all sorts of things if we were alone. *To the peasant woman:* Haven't you got something to do in the yard? The chickens to feed?

THE PEASANT WOMAN *falling suddenly to her knees:* Soldier, I didn't known anything about it. Please don't set my house on fire.

THE CORPORAL: What are you talking about?

THE PEASANT WOMAN: I have nothing to do with it. She left it on the doorstep, I swear.

THE CORPORAL *suddenly sees the child and whistles:* Ah, there's a little one in the crib! Blockhead, I smell a thousand piastres. Take the old girl out and hold on to her. It looks as though I'll have to do some cross-examining.

The peasant woman lets herself be led out by the soldier, without a word.

Well, there's the child I wanted to have from you. *He walks towards the crib.*

GRUSHA: Officer, it's mine. It's not the one you're after.

THE CORPORAL: I'll just have a look at it. *He bends over the crib. Grusha looks round in despair.*

GRUSHA: It's mine! It's mine!

THE CORPORAL: Nice linen!

Grusha jumps at him to pull him away. He throws her off and again bends over the crib. Looking round in despair, she suddenly sees a big log of wood, seizes it in panic, and hits the Corporal over the head from behind. She quickly picks up the child and dashes off.

THE SINGER

> After her escape from the Ironshirts
> After twenty-two days of wandering
> At the foot of the Janga-Tau glacier
> From this moment Grusha Vachnadze decided to be the
>   child's mother.

THE MUSICIANS

> The helpless girl
> Became the mother of the helpless child.

Grusha squats over a half-frozen stream to ladle some water in her hand for the child.

GRUSHA

> Nobody wants to take you
> So I shall have to take you
> There is no-one else but me, my dear
> On this black day in a meagre year
> Who will not forsake you.
>
> Since I've carried you too long
> And with sore feet
> Since the milk was too dear
> I grew fond of you.
> (I wouldn't be without you any more.)
>
> I'll throw your fine little shirt away
> And wrap you in rags
> I'll wash you and christen you
> With glacier water.
> (You'll have to bear it.)

She has taken off the child's fine linen and wrapped it in a rag.

THE SINGER

> When Grusha Vachnadze, pursued by the Ironshirts
> Came to the narrow footbridge of the Eastern slope
> She sang the song of the rotten bridge
> And risked two lives.

A wind has risen. The bridge on the glacier is visible in the semi-darkness. One rope is broken, and half the bridge is hanging down the precipice. Merchants, two men and a woman, stand undecided before the bridge as Grusha and the child arrive. One man is trying to retrieve a hanging rope with a stick.

THE FIRST MAN: Take your time, young woman. You won't get over that pass anyway.

GRUSHA: But I simply have to get my child over to the east side. To my brother.

THE MERCHANT WOMAN: Have to? What d'you mean by have to? I have to get there, too—because I have to buy two carpets in Atum—carpets a woman had to sell because her husband had to die. But can I do what I have to; can she? Andrei has been fishing for two hours for that rope. And I ask you, how are we to fasten it, even if he gets it?

THE FIRST MAN *listening:* Shush, I think I hear something.

GRUSHA: The bridge is not quite rotten. I think I'll try and cross it.

THE MERCHANT WOMAN: I wouldn't try that even if the devil himself were after me. It's suicide.

THE FIRST MAN *shouting:* Hi!

GRUSHA: Don't shout! *To the merchant woman.* Tell him not to shout.

THE FIRST MAN: But someone down there's calling. Perhaps they've lost their way.

THE MERCHANT WOMAN: And why shouldn't he shout? Is there something wrong with you? Are they after you?

GRUSHA: Well, I'll have to tell you. Ironshirts are after me. I knocked one down.

THE SECOND MAN: Hide our merchandise!

The woman hides a sack behind a rock.

THE FIRST MAN: Why didn't you tell us that at once? *To the other:* If they catch her they'll make mincemeat out of her!

GRUSHA: Get out of my way. I've got to cross that bridge.

THE SECOND MAN: You can't. There's a precipice of two thousand feet.

THE FIRST MAN: Even if we could get the rope it wouldn't make sense. We could hold it with our hands, but then the Ironshirts could get across in the same way.

GRUSHA: Out of my way.

Shouts from a distance: 'Let's get up there!'

THE MERCHANT WOMAN: They're getting near. But you can't take the child across that bridge. It's sure to break. Just look down!

Grusha looks down the precipice. The Ironshirts are heard shouting below.

THE SECOND MAN: Two thousand feet!

GRUSHA: But those men are worse.

THE FIRST MAN: Anyway you can't do it with the child. Risk your own life if they are after you, but not the child's.

THE SECOND MAN: She's even heavier with the child.

THE MERCHANT WOMAN: Perhaps she's really got to go. Give it to me. I'll hide it and you cross the bridge alone.

GRUSHA: I won't. We belong together. *To the child:* Live together, die together. *She sings:*

> If the gulf is deep
> And the rotten bridge sways
> It is not for us, son
> To choose our ways.
>
> The way that I know
> Is the one for your feet
> The bread that I find
> Is all you will eat.
>
> Of every four morsels
> You shall have three.
> I would that I knew
> How big they will be!

I'll try it.

THE MERCHANT WOMAN: That's tempting God.

Shouts from beneath.

GRUSHA: I beg you, throw that stick away, or they'll get the rope and follow me.

She starts off on to the swinging bridge. The merchant woman screams when the bridge looks like breaking. But Grusha walks on and reaches the far side.

THE FIRST MAN: She's done it!

THE MERCHANT WOMAN *who has fallen on her knees and begun to pray, angrily:* But I still think it was a sin.

The Ironshirts appear, the Corporal's head bandaged.

THE CORPORAL: Have you seen a woman with a child?

THE FIRST MAN *while the second throws away his stick:* Yes, there she is! But the bridge won't carry you!

THE CORPORAL: Blockhead, you'll suffer for this!

Grusha, from the far bank, laughs and shows the child to the Ironshirts. She walks on. The bridge is left behind. Wind.

GRUSHA *to the child:* You mustn't mind the wind. It's only a poor wretch, too. It has to push the clouds, and it feels the cold more than any of us. *Snow starts falling.* And the snow isn't the worst, Michael. It covers the little fir trees, so that they won't die in winter. And now I'll sing you a little song. Listen! *She sings:*

Your father's a thief
Your mother's a whore:
All the nice people
Will love you therefore.

The son of the tiger
Brings the foals their feed
The snake-child milk
To mothers in need.

4

IN THE NORTHERN MOUNTAINS

THE SINGER

Seven days the sister wandered.

Across the glacier, down the hills she wandered.

'When I enter my brother's house', she thought to herself

'He will rise and embrace me'.

'Is that you, sister?' he will say

'I have been expecting you for so long. This here is my
dear wife.

And this is my farm, come to me by marriage.

With eleven horses and thirty-one cows. Sit down.

Sit down with your child at our table and eat.'

The brother's house was in a lovely valley.

When the sister came to the brother she was ill from her
wanderings.

The brother rose from the table.

*A fat peasant couple who have just sat down to a meal. Lavrenti
Vachnadze already has a napkin round his neck, as Grusha, pale
and supported by a stableman, enters with the child.*

LAVRENTI: Where do you come from, Grusha?

GRUSHA *feebly:* I've walked across the Janga-Tau Pass,
Lavrenti.

STABLEMAN: I found her in front of the hay barn. She has a
child with her.

THE SISTER-IN-LAW: Go and groom the roan. *Exit stableman.*

LAVRENTI: This is my wife, Aniko.

THE SISTER-IN-LAW: We thought you were in service in
Nukha.

GRUSHA *barely able to stand:* Yes, I was there.

THE SISTER-IN-LAW: Wasn't it a good job? We were told it
was a good one.

GRUSHA: The Governor has been killed.

LAVRENTI: Yes, we heard there were riots. Your aunt told us about it. Remember, Aniko?

THE SISTER-IN-LAW: Here, with us, it's quiet. City people always need some kind of excitement. *She walks towards the door and shouts:* Sosso, Sosso, take the flat cake out of the oven, d'you hear? Where are you? *Exit, shouting.*

LAVRENTI *quietly, quickly:* Has it got a father? *As she shakes her head:* I thought so. We must think up something. She's very pious.

THE SISTER-IN-LAW *returning:* These servants! *To Grusha:* You have a child?

GRUSHA: It's mine. *She collapses. Lavrenti helps her up.*

THE SISTER-IN-LAW: Mary and Joseph, she's ill—what are wc to do?

Lavrenti tries to lead Grusha to the bench by the stove. Aniko waves her away in horror and points to the sack by the wall.

LAVRENTI *escorting her to the wall:* Sit down, sit down. I think it's just weakness.

THE SISTER-IN-LAW: As long as it's not scarlet fever.

LAVRENTI: Then she'd have spots. I'm sure it's only weakness. Don't worry, Aniko. *To Grusha:* Do you feel better sitting?

THE SISTER-IN-LAW: Is the child hers?

GRUSHA: It's mine.

LAVRENTI: She's on her way to her husband.

THE SISTER-IN-LAW: Really? Your meat's getting cold. *Lavrenti sits down and begins to eat.* Cold food's not good for you. At least the fat parts mustn't get cold; you know your stomach's your weak spot. *To Grusha:* If your husband's not in town, where is he then?

LAVRENTI: She got married on the other side of the mountain, she says.

THE SISTER-IN-LAW: Oh, on the other side. *She also sits down to eat.*

GRUSHA: I think I'll have to lie down somewhere, Lavrenti.

THE SISTER-IN-LAW *goes on questioning her:* If it's consumption we'll all get it. Has your husband a farm?

GRUSHA: He's a soldier.

LAVRENTI: But he's coming into a farm—a small farm from his father.

THE SISTER-IN-LAW: Isn't he in the war? Why not?

GRUSHA *wearily*: Yes, he's in the war.

THE SISTER-IN-LAW: Then why d'you want to go to the farm?

LAVRENTI: When he comes back from the war, he'll come to his farm.

THE SISTER-IN-LAW: But you're going there now?

LAVRENTI: Yes, to wait for him.

THE SISTER-IN-LAW *shrilly*: Sosso, the cake!

GRUSHA *murmurs in fever*: A farm—a soldier—waiting—sit down—eat.

THE SISTER-IN-LAW: That's scarlet fever.

GRUSHA *starting up*: Yes, he has a farm!

LAVRENTI: I think it must be weakness, Aniko. Wouldn't you like to go and look after the cake yourself, my dear?

THE SISTER-IN-LAW: But when will he come back if the war, as they say, has broken out again? *Waddling away, shouting*: Sosso! Where are you? Sosso!

LAVRENTI *getting up quickly and going to Grusha*: You'll get a bed in a moment. She has a good heart. But only after supper.

GRUSHA *holding out the child to him*: Take it. *He takes it, looking anxiously round*.

LAVRENTI: But you can't stay here long. You must realize she's very pious.

Grusha collapses. Lavrenti takes hold of her.

THE SINGER

　　The sister was too ill.
　　The cowardly brother had to give her shelter.
　　The autumn passed, the winter came.
　　The winter was long
　　The winter was short.
　　The people mustn't know.
　　The rats mustn't bite
　　The spring mustn't come.

Grusha sits bent at the weaving loom in the scullery. She and the child, who squats on the floor, are wrapped in blankets.

GRUSHA *sings while weaving:*

Then the lover started to leave
Then his girl ran pleading after him
Pleading and crying, crying and pleading:
Dearest mine, dearest mine
As you now go into battle
As you now have to fight the enemy
Don't throw yourself into the front line
And don't push with the rear line.
In front is red fire
In the rear is red smoke.
Stay wisely in between
Keep near the standard bearer.
The first ones always die
The last ones are also hit
Those in the centre come home.

Michael, we must be clever. If we make ourselves really small, like cockroaches, our sister-in-law will forget we're in the house. Then we can stay here till the snow melts. And don't cry because of the cold. Being poor and cold as well puts people off.

Enter Lavrenti. He sits down beside Grusha.

LAVRENTI: Why are you two sitting there muffled up like coachmen? Perhaps it's too cold in the room?

GRUSHA *hastily removing her shawl:* It's not too cold, Lavrenti.

LAVRENTI: If it's too cold, you oughtn't to sit here with the child. Aniko would blame herself. *Pause.* I hope the priest didn't question you about the child.

GRUSHA: He did, but I didn't tell him anything.

LAVRENTI: That's good. I wanted to talk to you about Aniko. She has a good heart—but she's very, very sensitive. People only have to mention our farm and she's worried. She takes everything to heart, you know. Our milkmaid once went to church with a hole in her stocking. Ever since then my dear Aniko has always worn two pairs of stockings to church. It's hard to believe, but it's the old family in her. *He listens.* Are you sure there are no rats here? If so, you couldn't stay here. *Sounds of drops from the roof.* What's that dripping?

GRUSHA: Must be a barrel leaking.

LAVRENTI: Yes, it must be a barrel. Now you've already been here six months, haven't you? Was I talking about Aniko? Of course I didn't mention the Ironshirt. She has a weak heart. That's why she doesn't know you can't look for work. And that's why she made those remarks yesterday. *They listen again to the melting snow.* Can you believe it? She's worrying about your soldier. 'Suppose he comes back and doesn't find her!' she says, and lies awake. 'He can't come before the spring,' I tell her. The dear woman! *The drops begin to fall faster.* When d'you think he'll come? What's your idea? *Grusha is silent.* Not before the spring. That's what you think, too? *Grusha is silent.* I see you no longer believe he'll come back. *Grusha does not answer.* But when spring comes and the snow is melting on the passes you must leave here. Because then they can come and look for you. People are already talking about a child with an unmarried mother.

The beat of the falling drops has grown faster and steadier.

Grusha, the snow is melting on the roof and spring is here.

GRUSHA: Yes.

LAVRENTI *eagerly:* Let me tell you what we'll do. You need a place to go to. And because of the child—*he sighs*—you must have a husband, to stop people talking. I've made cautious inquiries about how we can get a husband for you, Grusha, and I've found one. I talked to a woman who has a son, just over the mountain, a little farm. She's willing.

GRUSHA: But I can't marry another man! I must wait for Simon Chachava.

LAVRENTI: Of course. That's all been considered. You don't need a man in bed, but a man on paper. And that's the very man I've found. The son of the woman I spoke to is dying. Isn't that wonderful? He's just at his last gasp. And everything's as we have said: A man just over the mountain! And when you reached him he died, and so you're a widow. What do you say?

GRUSHA: I could do with a stamped up document for Michael.

LAVRENTI: A stamp makes all the difference. Without a stamp even the Shah of Persia couldn't prove he is the Shah. And you'll have a roof over your head.

GRUSHA: How much does she want for it?

LAVRENTI: 400 piastres.

GRUSHA: Where will you find the money?

LAVRENTI *guiltily:* Aniko's milk money.

GRUSHA: No-one will know us over there. I'll do it.

LAVRENTI *gets up:* I'll tell the woman at once. *Exit quickly.*

GRUSHA: Michael, you cause a lot of trouble. I came by you as the pear tree comes by the sparrows. And because a Christian bends down and picks up a crust of bread so it won't go to waste. Michael, I ought to have walked away quickly on that Easter Sunday in Nukha. Now I'm the fool.

THE SINGER

> The bridegroom was lying on his deathbed, when the bride arrived.
> The bridegroom's mother was waiting at the door, bidding them hurry.
> The bride brought along a child, the witness hid it during the wedding.

A space divided by a partition. On one side a bed. Under the mosquito net lies a very sick man. On the other side the mother-in-law rushes in pulling Grusha after her. They are followed by Lavrenti and the child.

THE MOTHER-IN-LAW: Quick! Quick! Or he'll die on us before the wedding. *To Lavrenti:* But I was never told she already had a child.

LAVRENTI: What's it matter? *Pointing towards the dying man:* It's all the same to him in his condition.

THE MOTHER-IN-LAW: Him? But I won't survive the shame. We're honest people. *She begins to weep.* My Yussup doesn't have to marry someone who already has a child.

LAVRENTI: All right, I'll add another 200 piastres. You have it in writing that the farm will go to you; but she has the right to live here for two years.

THE MOTHER-IN-LAW *drying her tears:* It will hardly cover the funeral expenses. I hope she will really lend me a hand with the work. And now what's happened to the monk? He must have slipped out by the kitchen window. When they get wind in the village that Yussup's end is near, they'll all be round our necks. Oh dear! I'll go and get the monk. But he mustn't see the child.

LAVRENTI: I'll take care he doesn't see it. But why a monk? Why not a priest?

THE MOTHER-IN-LAW: Oh, he's just as good. I made one mistake: I paid him half his fee in advance. Now he'll have gone to the tavern. I hope . . . *She runs off.*

LAVRENTI: She saved on the priest, the wretch! She's hired a cheap monk.

GRUSHA: Send Simon Chachava to me if he turns up.

LAVRENTI: Yes. *Glancing at the sick man:* Won't you have a look at him?

Grusha, taking Michael to her, shakes her head.

He's not moving an eyelid. I hope we aren't too late.

They listen. On the opposite side enter neighbours, who look round and take up positions against the walls. They start muttering prayers. Enter the mother-in-law with the monk.

THE MOTHER-IN-LAW *surprised and angry, to the monk:* Now we're for it! *She bows to the guests.* I must ask you to wait a few moments. My son's bride has just arrived from town and we've got to have an emergency wedding. *She goes with the monk into the bedchamber.* I knew you'd spread it about. *To Grusha:* The wedding can start at once. Here's the licence. I and the bride's brother—*Lavrenti tries to hide in the background, after having quickly taken Michael away from Grusha.*

The mother-in law beckons him away from the child—the bride's brother and I are the witnesses.

Grusha has bowed to the monk. They approach the bed: the mother-in-law lifts the mosquito-net: the monk begins babbling the marriage service in Latin. Meanwhile the mother-in-law beckons to Lavrenti to get rid of the child, but Lavrenti, fearing that the child will cry, draws its attention to the ceremony. Grusha glances once at the child, and Lavrenti makes the child wave to her.

THE MONK: Are you prepared to be a faithful, obedient and good wife to this man? And to cleave to him until death you do part?

GRUSHA *looking at the child:* Yes.

THE MONK *to the dying man:* And are you prepared to be a good and loving husband to your wife until death you do part?

As the dying man does not answer, the monk repeats the question, then looks round.

THE MOTHER-IN-LAW: Of course he is! Didn't you hear him say yes?

THE MONK: All right. We declare this marriage contracted. Now what about Extreme Unction?

THE MOTHER-IN-LAW: Nothing doing! The wedding was quite expensive enough. I must now take care of the mourners. *To Lavrenti:* Did we say 700?

LAVRENTI: 600. *He pays.* Now I don't want to sit and get acquainted with the guests. So farewell, Grusha. And if my widowed sister comes to visit me one day, she'll get a 'welcome' from my wife. Or I'll get disagreeable.

He leaves. The mourners glance after him without interest.

THE MONK: And may one ask whose this child is?

THE MOTHER-IN-LAW: Is there a child? I don't see any child. And you don't see one either—understand? Or else I've seen all kinds of things happening behind the tavern! Come along now.

They move back to the room. After Grusha has put down the child and told it to be quiet, she is introduced to the neighbours.

This is my daughter-in-law. She arrived just in time to find dear Yussup still alive.

ONE OF THE WOMEN: He's been ill now a whole year, hasn't he? When my Vassili was called up he was there to say goodbye.

ANOTHER WOMAN: Such things are terrible for a farm. With the corn ripe on the stalk and the farmer in bed! It will be a blessing for him if he doesn't suffer much longer, I say.

FIRST WOMAN *confidentially:* At first we thought he took to his bed because of military service, you know. And now his end is coming.

THE MOTHER-IN-LAW: Please sit down and have some cakes. *She beckons to Grusha and both women go into the bedroom, where they pick up trays of cakes from the floor. The guests, among them the monk, sit on the floor and begin conversing in subdued voices.*

A VERY OLD PEASANT *to whom the monk has slipped the bottle he has taken from his cassock:* There's a little one, you say! How can Yussup have managed that?

THIRD WOMAN: Anyway, she was lucky to have brought it off in time, with him so sick.

THE MOTHER-IN-LAW: They are gossiping already. And stuffing themselves with the funeral cakes at the same time. And if he doesn't die today, I'll have to bake fresh ones tomorrow.

GRUSHA: I'll bake them.

THE MOTHER-IN-LAW: When some riders passed by last night, and I went out to see who they were, he was lying there like a corpse! That's why I sent for you. It can't take much longer. *She listens.*

THE MONK: Dear wedding guests and mourners! We stand deeply moved in front of a bed of death and marriage, because the bride gets into bed and the groom into the grave. The groom is already washed, and the bride is already hot. For in the marriage-bed lies the last Will, and that makes people randy. Oh, my children, how varied is the fate of man! The one dies to get a roof over his head, and the other marries so that flesh may be turned to dust, from which it was made. Amen.

THE MOTHER-IN-LAW *who had listened:* He's got his own

back. I shouldn't have hired such a cheap one. That's what you'd expect. An expensive one knows how to behave. In Sura there's one who is even in the odour of sanctity; but of course he charges a fortune. A fifty-piastre priest like this one here has no dignity. And as for piety, he has precisely fifty piastres' worth, and no more. And when I fetched him from the tavern he was just finishing a speech and shouting: 'The war is over, beware of the peace!' We must go in.

GRUSHA *giving Michael a cake:* Eat this cake and be a good boy, Michael. We are respectable now.

The two women carry the trays of cakes to the guests. The dying man is sitting up in bed; he puts his head out from under the mosquito-net and watches the two women. Then he sinks back again. The monk takes two bottles from his cassock and offers them to the peasant beside him. Enter three musicians, to whom the monk waves with a grin.

THE MOTHER-IN-LAW *to the musicians:* What have you got your instruments for?

A MUSICIAN: Brother Anastasius here—*pointing at the monk*—told us there was a wedding going on.

THE MOTHER-IN-LAW: What! You brought them? Three more on my neck! Don't you know there's a dying man next door?

THE MONK: That's a tempting task for an artist. They could play a hushed Wedding March or a gay Funeral Dance.

THE MOTHER-IN-LAW: Well, you might as well play. I can't stop you eating, in any case.

The musicians play a musical medley. The women offer cakes.

THE MONK: The trumpet sounds like a whining baby. And you, little drum, what gossip are you spreading abroad?

A PEASANT *beside the monk:* What about the bride shaking a leg?

THE MONK: Shake the legs or rattle the bones?

THE PEASANT *beside the monk, singing:*

When pretty Miss Plushbottom wed
A rich man with no teeth in his head

They enquired, 'Is it fun?'
She replied, 'No, it's none.
Still, there're candles and soon he'll be dead.'

The mother-in-law throws the drunken man out. The music stops. The guests are embarrassed. Pause.

THE GUESTS *loudly:* Have you heard the latest? The Grand Duke's back!—But the Princes are against him.—Oh, the Shah of Persia, they say, has lent him a great army, to restore order in Grusinia.—How is this possible? After all, the Shah of Persia is against the Grand Duke!—But against disorder, too.—In any case, the war's over. Our soldiers are already coming back.

Grusha drops the tray of cakes.

AN OLD WOMAN *to Grusha:* Are you feeling ill? That's just excitement about dear Yussup. Sit down and rest awhile, my dear.

Grusha stands, swaying.

THE GUESTS: Now everything will be as it was. Only the taxes will go up because we'll have to pay for the war.

GRUSHA *weakly:* Did someone say the soldiers are back?

A MAN: I did.

GRUSHA: That can't be true.

THE MAN *to a woman:* Show her the shawl. We bought it from a soldier. It's from Persia.

GRUSHA *looking at the shawl:* They are here.

A long pause. Grusha kneels as if to pick up the cakes. As she does so she takes the silver cross and chain out of her blouse, kisses it, and starts praying.

THE MOTHER-IN-LAW *while the guests silently watch Grusha:* What's the matter with you? Won't you look after our guests? What's all this nonsense from the city got to do with us?

THE GUESTS *resuming their conversation while Grusha remains with her forehead bent to the ground:* Persian saddles can be bought from soldiers, but some exchange them for crutches.— Only one side's bigwigs can win, but the soldiers on both sides are the losers.—At least the war's over now.

It's something that they can't call you up any more.—*The dying man sits bolt upright in bed. He listens.*—What we need most are two weeks of good weather.—There's hardly a pear on our trees this year.

THE MOTHER-IN-LAW *offering the cakes:* Have some more cake. And enjoy it. There's more to come.

The mother-in-law goes to the bedroom with empty trays. Unaware of the dying man, she bends down to pick up some more cakes, when he begins to talk in a hoarse voice.

YUSSUP: How many more cakes are you going to stuff down their throats? D'you think I can shit money? *The mother-in-law starts, and stares at him aghast, while he puts his head out from behind the mosquito-net.* Did they say the war was over?

FIRST WOMAN *talking kindly to Grusha in the next room:* Has the young woman someone in the war?

THE MAN: That's good news that they're on their way home, eh?

YUSSUP: Don't stare so! Where's the wife you've foisted on me?

Receiving no answer, he climbs out of bed and in his nightshirt staggers past his mother into the other room. Trembling, she follows him with the cake tray.

THE GUESTS *seeing him and shrieking:* Jesus, Mary and Joseph! Yussup!

Everyone leaps up in alarm. The women rush to the door. Grusha, still on her knees, turns round and stares at the man.

YUSSUP: The funeral supper! That's what you'd like! Get out before I kick you out!

The guests stampede from the house.

YUSSUP *grumpily to Grusha:* That puts a spoke in your wheel, eh?

Receiving no answer, he turns round and takes a cake from the tray which his mother holds.

THE SINGER

Oh, confusion! The wife discovers that she has a husband!

By day there's the child, by night there's the man.

The lover is on his way day and night.

The married couple are looking at each other. The chamber is narrow.

Yussup sits naked in a high wooden bathtub. His mother pours water from a jug. Next door in the bedroom Grusha squats with Michael, who is playing at mending a straw mat.

YUSSUP: That's her business, not yours. Where's she hiding now?

THE MOTHER-IN-LAW *calling:* Grusha! The peasant wants you!

GRUSHA *to Michael:* There are still two holes to mend.

YUSSUP *as Grusha enters:* Scrub my back!

GRUSHA: Can't the peasant do that himself?

YUSSUP: 'Can't the peasant do that himself?' Get the brush! To hell with you! Are you the wife or are you a stranger? *To the mother-in-law:* Too cold!

THE MOTHER-IN-LAW: I'll run and get some more hot water.

GRUSHA: Let me do it.

YUSSUP: You stay here. *The mother-in-law goes out.* Rub harder. And don't make such a fuss. You've seen a naked man before. That child of yours can't have come out of thin air.

GRUSHA: The child was not conceived in joy, if that's what the peasant means.

YUSSUP *turning and grinning:* A likely story! *Grusha stops scrubbing him and starts back. Enter the mother-in-law.* This is a nice thing you've saddled me with here! A cold-fish for a wife!

THE MOTHER-IN-LAW: She isn't willing.

YUSSUP: Pour—but go easy! Ow! Go easy, I said. *To Grusha.* I'd be surprised if you hadn't been up to something in the city. What else would you be here for? But I won't say anything about that. I also haven't said anything about the bastard you brought into my house. But my patience with you is coming to an end. It's against nature. *To the mother-in-law:* More! *To Grusha:* And even if your soldier does return, you're married.

GRUSHA: Yes.

YUSSUP: But your soldier won't return now. Don't you believe it.

GRUSHA: No.

YUSSUP: You're cheating me. You're my wife and you're not my wife. Where you lie, nothing lies. And yet no other woman can lie there. When I go to work in the mornings I'm dead-tired. When I lie down at night I'm awake as the devil. God has made you a woman, and what d'you do about it? My fields don't bring me in enough to buy myself a woman in town. Besides, it's a long way. Woman hoes the fields and parts her legs. That's what our almanac says. D'you hear?

GRUSHA: Yes. *Quietly.* I don't like cheating you out of it.

YUSSUP: She doesn't like! Pour some more water. *The mother-in-law pours.* Ow!

THE SINGER

  As she sat by the stream to wash the linen
  She saw his image in the water, and his face grew dimmer
  As the months passed by.
  As she raised herself to wring the linen
  She heard his voice from the murmuring maple, and his voice grew fainter
  As the months passed by.
  Excuses and sighs grew more numerous, tears and sweat flowed faster
  As the months passed by, as the child grew up.

Grusha sits by a stream dipping linen into the water. Some distance away a few children are standing. Grusha is talking to Michael.

GRUSHA: You can play with them, Michael. But don't let them order you about because you're the smallest.

Michael nods and joins the children. They start playing.

THE TALLEST BOY: Today we're going to play Heads-off. *To a fat boy:* You're the Prince and you must laugh. *To Michael:* You're the Governor. *To a girl:* You're the Governor's wife and you cry when his head's chopped off. And I do the chopping. *He shows his wooden sword.* With this. First, the Governor's led into the courtyard. The Prince walks ahead. The Governor's wife comes last.

They form a procession. The fat boy goes ahead, and laughs. Then comes Michael, and the tallest boy, and then the girl, who weeps.

MICHAEL *standing still:* Me too chop head off!

THE TALLEST BOY: That's my job. You're the smallest. The Governor's part is easiest. All you do is kneel down and have your head chopped off. That's simple.

MICHAEL: Me too have sword.

THE TALLEST BOY: That's mine. *He gives him a kick.*

THE GIRL *shouting to Grusha:* He doesn't want to do what he's told.

GRUSHA *laughing:* Even ducklings take to water, they say.

THE TALLEST BOY: You can play the Prince if you know how to laugh.

Michael shakes his head.

THE FAT BOY: I'm the best laugher. Let him chop off the head just once. Then you do it, then me.

Reluctantly the tallest boy hands Michael the wooden sword and kneels. The fat boy sits down, smacks his thigh and laughs with all his might. The girl weeps loudly. Michael swings the big sword and chops off the head. In doing so, he topples over.

THE TALLEST BOY: Hi, I'll show you how to do it properly.

Michael runs away, and the children run after him. Grusha laughs, following them with her eyes. On turning round, she sees Simon Chachava standing on the opposite bank. He wears a shabby uniform.

GRUSHA: Simon!

SIMON: Is that Grusha Vachnadze?

GRUSHA: Simon!

SIMON *politely:* A good morning, and good health to the young lady.

GRUSHA *gets up gaily and bows deeply:* A good morning to the soldier. And thank God he has returned in good health.

SIMON: They found better fish than me, so they didn't eat me, said the haddock.

GRUSHA: Courage, said the kitchen boy. Luck, said the hero.

SIMON: And how are things here? Was the winter bearable? Did the neighbour behave?

GRUSHA: The winter was a little rough, the neighbour as usual, Simon.

SIMON: May one ask if a certain person is still in the habit of putting her leg in the water when washing her linen?

GRUSHA: The answer is no. Because of the eyes in the bushes.

SIMON: The young lady is talking about soldiers. Here stands a paymaster.

GRUSHA: Is that worth twenty piastres?

SIMON: And board.

GRUSHA *with tears in her eyes:* Behind the barracks under the date trees.

SIMON: Just there. I see someone has kept her eyes open.

GRUSHA: Someone has.

SIMON: And has not forgotten. *Grusha shakes her head.* And so the door is still on its hinges, as they say. *Grusha looks at him in silence and shakes her head again.* What's that mean? Is something wrong?

GRUSHA: Simon Chachava, I can never go back to Nukha. Something has happened.

SIMON: What has happened?

GRUSHA: It so happened that I knocked down an Ironshirt.

SIMON: Grusha Vachnadze will have had her reasons for that.

GRUSHA: Simon Chachava, my name is also no longer what it was.

SIMON *after a pause:* I don't understand that.

GRUSHA: When do women change their names, Simon? Let me explain it to you: Nothing stands between us. Everything between us has remained as it was. You've got to believe that.

SIMON: How can nothing stand between us and things be changed?

GRUSHA: How can I explain it to you? So fast and with the stream between us? Couldn't you cross that bridge?

SIMON: Perhaps it's no longer necessary.

GRUSHA: It's most necessary. Come over, Simon. Quick!

SIMON: Is the young lady saying that someone has come too late?

Grusha looks up at him in despair, her face streaming with tears. Simon stares before him. He picks up a piece of wood and starts cutting it.

THE SINGER

> So many words are said, so many words are left unsaid.
> The soldier has come. Whence he comes he doesn't say.
> Hear what he thought but didn't say:
> The battle began at dawn, grew bloody at noon.
> The first fell before me, the second behind me, the third at my side.
> I trod on the first, I abandoned the second, the captain sabred the third.
> My one brother died by steel, my other brother died by smoke.
> My neck was burnt by fire, my hands froze in my gloves, my toes in my socks.
> For food I had aspen buds, for drink I had maple brew, for bed I had stones in water.

SIMON: I see a cap in the grass. Is there a little one already?

GRUSHA: There is, Simon. How could I hide it? But please don't let it worry you. It's not mine.

SIMON: They say: Once the wind begins to blow, it blows through every crack. The woman need say no more.

Grusha lowers her head and says no more.

THE SINGER

> There was great yearning but there was no waiting.
> The oath is broken. Why was not disclosed.
> Hear what she thought, but didn't say:
> While you fought in the battle, soldier
> The bloody battle, the bitter battle
> I found a child who was helpless
> And hadn't the heart to do away with it.
> I had to care for what otherwise would have come to harm

I had to bend down on the floor for breadcrumbs
I had to tear myself to pieces for what was not mine
But alien.
Someone must be the helper.
Because the little tree needs its water
The little lamb loses its way when the herdsman is asleep
And the bleating remains unheard.

SIMON: Give me back the cross I gave you. Or better, throw
it in the stream.
He turns to go.

GRUSHA: Simon Chachava, don't go away. It isn't mine, it
isn't mine! *She hears the children calling.* What is it, children?

VOICES: Soldiers have come!—They are taking Michael
away!
*Grusha stands aghast as two Ironshirts, with Michael between
them, come towards her.*

IRONSHIRT: Are you Grusha? *She nods.* Is that your child?

GRUSHA: Yes. *Simon goes off.* Simon!

IRONSHIRT: We have official orders to take this child, found
in your charge, back to the city. There is suspicion that it is
Michael Abashvili, son and heir of the late Governor Georgi
Abashvili, and his wife, Natella Abashvili. Here is the
document and the seal.
They lead the child away.

GRUSHA *running after them and shouting:* Leave it here, please!
It's mine!

THE SINGER
The Ironshirts took the child away, the precious child.
The unhappy girl followed them to the city, the danger-
ous place.
The real mother demanded the child back. The foster
mother faced her trial.
Who will try the case, on whom will the child be be-
stowed?
Who will be the Judge? A good one, a bad one?
The city was in flames. On the Judgment Seat sat Azdak.

5

THE STORY OF THE JUDGE

THE SINGER
Listen now to the story of the Judge:
How he turned Judge, how he passed judgment, what kind of Judge he is.
On the Easter Sunday of the great revolt, when the Grand Duke was overthrown
And his Governor Abashvili, father of our child, lost his head
The village clerk Azdak found a fugitive in the woods and hid him in his hut.

Azdak, in rags and tipsy, helps a fugitive dressed as a beggar into his hut.

AZDAK: Don't snort. You're not a horse. And it won't do you any good with the police if you run like a dirty nose in April. Stop, I tell you. *He catches the fugitive, who has trotted into the hut as though he would go through the walls.* Sit down and feed: here's a piece of cheese. *From under some rags in a chest he fishes out some cheese, and the fugitive greedily begins to eat.* Haven't had anything for some time, eh? *The fugitive groans.* Why did you run so fast, you arse-hole? The police wouldn't even have seen you!

THE FUGITIVE: Had to.

AZDAK: Blue funk? *The fugitive stares, uncomprehending.* Got the squitters? Afraid? Don't slobber like a Grand Duke or a sow. I can't stand it. It's well-born stinkers we've got to put up with as God made them. Not the likes of you. I once heard of a Senior Judge who farted at a public dinner. Just to show his independence. Watching you eat like that really gives me the most awful ideas! Why don't you say something? *Sharply.* Let's have a look at your hand. Can't you hear? Show me your hand. *The fugitive slowly puts out his hand.* White! So you're no beggar at all! A fraud! A swindle

on legs! And here am I hiding you from the police as though
you were a decent human being! Why run like that if you're
a landowner? Because that's what you are. Don't try to
deny it. I see it in your guilty face. *He gets up.* Get out of
here! *The fugitive looks uncertainly at him.* What are you waiting
for, you peasant-flogger?

THE FUGITIVE: Am hunted. Ask for undivided attention.
Make proposition.

AZDAK: What do you want to make? A proposition? Well, if
that isn't the height of insolence! He making a proposition!
The bitten man scratches his fingers bloody, and the leech
makes a proposition. Get out, I tell you!

THE FUGITIVE: Understand point of view. Persuasion. Will
pay 100,000 piastres for one night. How's that?

AZDAK: What? Do you think you can buy me? And for
100,000 piastres? A third-rate farm. Let's say 150,000. Got
it?

THE FUGITIVE: Not on me, of course. Will be sent. Hope,
don't doubt.

AZDAK: Doubt profoundly! Get out!
The fugitive gets up and trots to the door. A voice from off-stage.

VOICE: Azdak!
The fugitive turns, trots to the opposite corner and stands still.

AZDAK *shouting:* I'm not in. *He walks to the door.* Is that you
spying around here again, Shauva?

POLICEMAN SHAUVA *outside, reproachfully:* You've snared
another rabbit, Azdak. You promised me it wouldn't
happen again.

AZDAK *severely:* Shauva, don't talk about things you don't
understand. The rabbit is a dangerous and destructive
animal. It devours plants, especially what they call weeds.
So it must be exterminated.

SHAUVA: Azdak, don't be so hard on me. I'll lose my job if I
don't arrest you. I know you have a good heart.

AZDAK: I *don't* have a good heart! How often am I to tell you
I'm a man of intellect?

SHAUVA *slyly:* I know, Azdak. You're a superior person. You say so yourself. I'm a Christian and I've no education. So I ask you: if one of the Prince's rabbits is stolen, and I'm a policeman, what am I to do with the offender?

AZDAK: Shauva, Shauva, shame on you! There you stand asking me a question. Nothing is more tempting than a question. Suppose you were a woman—let's say Nunovna, that bad girl—and you showed me your thigh—Nunovna's thigh, that is—and you asked me: what shall I do with my thigh? It itches. Is she as innocent as she pretends? No. I catch a rabbit, you catch a man. Man is made in God's image. Not so a rabbit, you know that. I'm a rabbit-eater; but you're a man-eater, Shauva. And God will pass judgment on you. Shauva, go home and repent. No, stop! There's something . . . *He looks at the fugitive, who stands trembling in the corner.* No, it's nothing after all. Go home and repent. *He slams the door behind Shauva. To the fugitive:* Now you're surprised, eh? Surprised I didn't hand you over? But I couldn't hand over even a bedbug to that beast of a policeman! It goes against my grain. Don't tremble at the sight of a policeman. So old and yet so cowardly! Finish your cheese, but eat it like a poor man, or else they'll still catch you. Do I even have to tell you how a poor man behaves? *He makes him sit down, and then gives him back the cheese.* The box is the table. Put your elbows on the table, and now surround the plate with your arms as though you expected the cheese to be snatched from you at any moment. What right have you to be safe? Now hold the knife as if it were a small sickle; and don't look so greedily at your cheese, look at it mournfully—because it's already disappearing—like all good things. *Azdak watches him.* They're after you. That speaks in your favour. But how can I be sure they're not mistaken about you? In Tiflis they once hanged a landowner, a Turk. He could prove he quartered his peasants instead of merely cutting them in half, as is the custom. And he squeezed twice the usual amount of taxes out of them. His zeal was above all suspicion, and yet they hanged him like a common criminal. Why? Because he was a Turk—something he couldn't do much about. An injustice! He got on to the gallows like Pontius Pilate into the Creed. In a word, I don't trust you.

THE SINGER

Thus Azdak gave shelter to the old beggar

Only to find out that he was that murderer, the Grand Duke.

And he was ashamed of himself, he accused himself and ordered the policeman

To take him to Nukha, to Court, to be judged.

In the Court of Justice three Ironshirts sit drinking. From a pillar hangs a man in judge's robes. Enger Azdak, in chains, dragging Shauva behind him.

AZDAK *shouting:* I have helped the Grand Duke, the Grand Thief, the Grand Murderer, to escape! In the name of Justice, I demand to be judged severely in a public trial!

THE FIRST IRONSHIRT: Who is this queer bird?

SHAUVA: That's our clerk, Azdak.

AZDAK: I am despicable, treacherous, branded! Tell them, flatfoot, how I insisted on being put in chains and brought to the capital. Because I sheltered the Grand Duke, the Grand Swindler, by mistake. As I realized only afterwards when I found this document in my hut. *The Ironshirts study the document. To Shauva:* They can't read. Point out that the branded man is accusing himself. Tell them how I forced you to walk with me through half the night, to get everything cleared up.

SHAUVA: And all by threats. That wasn't nice of you, Azdak.

AZDAK: Shauva, shut your trap. You don't understand. A new age has come, which will thunder over you. You're finished. The police are being wiped out, pfft! Everything is being investigated, brought into the open. In which case a man prefers to give himself up. Why? Because he won't escape the mob. Tell them how I've been shouting all along Shoemaker Street! *He acts with expansive gestures, looking sideways at the Ironshirts.* 'Out of ignorance I let the

Grand Swindler escape. Tear me to pieces, brothers!' So as
to get in first.

THE FIRST IRONSHIRT: And what was their answer?

SHAUVA: They comforted him in Butcher Street, and laughed
themselves sick in Shoemaker Street. That's all.

AZDAK: But here with you it's different, I know you're men
of iron. Brothers, where is the Judge? I must be tried.

THE FIRST IRONSHIRT *pointing at the hanged man:* Here's the
Judge. And stop 'brothering' us. That's rather a sore spot
this evening.

AZDAK: 'Here's the Judge.' That's an answer never heard in
Grusinia before. Citizens, where's His Excellency the
Governor? *Pointing at the gallows:* Here's His Excellency,
stranger. Where's the Chief Tax Collector? Where's the
official Recruiting Officer? The Patriarch? The Chief of
Police? Here, here, here—all here. Brothers, that's what I
expected from you.

THE SECOND IRONSHIRT: Stop! What did you expect, you
bird?

AZDAK: What happened in Persia, brothers. What happened
there.

THE SECOND IRONSHIRT: And what did happen in Persia?

AZDAK: Forty years ago. Everyone hanged. Viziers, tax-
collectors. My grandfather, a remarkable man, saw it all.
For three whole days. Everywhere.

THE SECOND IRONSHIRT: And who reigned after the Vizier
was hanged?

AZDAK: A peasant.

THE SECOND IRONSHIRT: And who commanded the army?

AZDAK: A soldier, soldier.

THE SECOND IRONSHIRT: And who paid the wages?

ADAZK: A dyer. A dyer paid the wages.

THE SECOND IRONSHIRT: Wasn't it a carpet weaver perhaps?

THE FIRST IRONSHIRT: And why did all this happen, you
Persian?

AZDAK: 'Why did all this happen?' Must there be a special

reason? Why do you scratch yourself, brother? War! Too long a war! And no justice! My grandfather brought back a song that tells what it was all about. I and my friend the policeman will sing it for you. *To Shauva:* And hold on to the rope, that's part of it. *He sings, with Shauva holding the rope.*

Why don't our sons bleed any longer, why don't our daughters weep any more?

Why do only the calves in the slaughterhouse have any blood, why only willows on Lake Urmi tears?

The Grand King must have a new province, the peasant must relinquish his savings.

In order to capture the roof of the world, the cottage roofs have to be torn down.

Our men are scattered in all directions, so that the great ones can eat at home.

The soldiers kill each other, the marshals salute each other.

The widow's tax money has to be fingered to see if it's good, the swords break.

The battle has been lost, but the helmets have been paid for.

Is that right? Is that right?

SHAUVA: Yes, yes, yes, yes, yes, that's right.

AZDAK: Do you want to hear the whole thing?

The first Ironshirt nods.

THE SECOND IRONSHIRT *to Shauva:* Did he teach you that song?

SHAUVA: Yes. Only my voice isn't good.

THE SECOND IRONSHIRT: No. *To Azdak:* Go on singing.

AZDAK: The second verse is about the peace. *He sings:*

The offices are jammed, the officials are working in the streets.

The rivers overflow their banks and lay waste the fields.

Those incapable of letting down their own trousers rule countries.

Those who can't count up to four devour eight courses.

The corn farmers look round for buyers, but see only the
  starving.

The weavers go home from their looms in rags.

Is that right? Is that right?

SHAUVA: Yes, yes, yes, yes, yes, that's right.

AZDAK:

That's why our sons bleed no longer, our daughters weep
  no more.

That's why only the calves in the slaughterhouse have
  any blood.

And the willows in the morning on Lake Urmi have any
  tears.

THE FIRST IRONSHIRT *after a pause:* Are you going to sing
that song here in town?

AZDAK: Of course. What's wrong with it?

THE FIRST IRONSHIRT: Do you see the sky getting red?
Turning round, Azdak sees the sky reddened by fire. That's in the
outer town. This morning when Prince Kazbeki had Governor Abashvili beheaded our carpet weavers also caught the
'Persian disease'. They asked if Prince Kazbeki isn't eating
too many courses. And this afternoon they strung up the
town judge. But we beat them to pulp for two piastres per
weaver, you understand?

AZDAK *after a pause:* I understand.
*He glances shyly round and, creeping away, sits down in a corner, his
head in his hands.*

THE FIRST IRONSHIRT *to the third, after they have all had a
drink:* Just wait and see what'll happen next.
*The first and second Ironshirts walk towards Azdak and block his
exit.*

SHAUVA: I don't think he's a really bad character, gentlemen.
He poaches a few chickens here and there, and perhaps an
odd rabbit.

THE SECOND IRONSHIRT *approaching Azdak:* You've come
here to fish in troubled waters, eh?

AZDAK *looking up:* I don't know why I've come here.

THE SECOND IRONSHIRT: Do you happen to be in with the

carpet weavers? *Azdak shakes his head.* And what about this song?

AZDAK: From my grandfather. A stupid, ignorant man.

THE SECOND IRONSHIRT: Right. And what about the dyer who paid the wages?

AZDAK: That was in Persia.

THE FIRST IRONSHIRT: And what about denouncing yourself for not having hanged the Grand Duke with your own hands?

AZDAK: Didn't I tell you that I let him escape?

SHAUVA: I swear to it. He let him escape.

The Ironshirts drag Azdak screaming to the gallows. Then they let him loose and burst out laughing. Azdak joins in the laughter, laughing loudest. They then unchain him. They all start drinking. Enter the fat prince with a young man.

THE FIRST IRONSHIRT *to Azdak:* There you have your new age.

More laughter.

THE FAT PRINCE: And what is there to laugh about here, my friends? Permit me a serious word. Yesterday morning the Princes of Grusinia overthrew the Grand Duke's war-thirsty government and did away with his governors. Unfortunately the Grand Duke himself escaped. In this fateful hour our carpet weavers, these eternal trouble-makers, had the audacity to incite a rebellion and hang our universally beloved city Judge, our dear Illa Orbeliani. Tut-tut. My friends, we need peace, peace, peace in Grusinia. And justice. Here I bring you my dear nephew, Bizergan Kazbeki. He's to be the new Judge, a talented fellow. I say: the people must decide.

THE FIRST IRONSHIRT: Does this mean we elect the Judge?

THE FAT PRINCE: Precisely. The people propose a talented fellow. Confer, my friends. *The Ironshirts confer.* Don't worry, little fox. The job's yours. And once we've run the Grand Duke to earth we won't have to kiss the rabble's arse any more.

THE IRONSHIRTS *to each other:* They've got the jitters because they still haven't caught the Grand Duke.—We've this clerk to thank for that. He let him get away.—They're not sure of things yet. So they say: 'My friends!' And: 'The people must decide!'—Now he even wants justice for Grusinia!—But fun's fun as long as it lasts.—We'll ask the clerk; he knows all about justice. Hey, scoundrel . . .

AZDAK: You mean me?

THE FIRST IRONSHIRT *continues:* Would you like to have the nephew as Judge?

AZDAK: You asking me? You're not really asking me that, are you?

THE SECOND IRONSHIRT: Why not? Anything for a laugh!

AZDAK: I take it you want him put to the test? Am I right? Have you a crook on hand? An experienced one? So the candidate can show how good he is?

THE THIRD IRONSHIRT: Let me see. We have the Governor's tarts' two doctors down there. Let's use them.

AZDAK: Stop! That's no good! You can't take real crooks till we're sure of the Judge being appointed. He may be an ass, but he must be appointed or else the law is violated. The law is a very sensitive organ. Like the spleen. Once attacked with fists, death occurs. You can hang those two. Why not? You won't have violated the law, because no Judge was present. Judgment must always be passed with complete solemnity—because it's such rot. Suppose a Judge throws a woman into clink for having stolen a corncake for her child. And he isn't wearing his robes. Or he's scratching himself while passing sentence so that more than a third of his body is exposed—in which case he'd have to scratch his thigh—then the sentence he passes is a disgrace and the law is violated. It would be easier for a Judge's robe and a Judge's hat to pass sentence than for a man without all that paraphernalia. If you don't look out, the law goes up in smoke. You don't taste wine by offering it to a dog. Why not? Because the wine would be gone.

THE FIRST IRONSHIRT: So what do you suggest, you hair-splitter?

AZDAK: I'll be the defendant. I even know what sort. *Azdak whispers to them.*

THE FIRST IRONSHIRT: You? *All burst out laughing.*

THE FAT PRINCE: What have you decided?

THE FIRST IRONSHIRT: We've decided to have a rehearsal. Our good friend will act as defendant, and here's the Judge's seat for the candidate.

THE FAT PRINCE: That's unusual. But why not? *To the nephew:* A mere formality, little fox. What did they teach you? Who gets there first? The slow runner or the fast one?

THE NEPHEW: The silent one, Uncle Arsen.

The nephew sits in the Judge's seat, the fat prince standing behind him. The Ironshirts sit on the steps. Enter Azdak, imitating the unmistakeable gait of the Grand Duke.

AZDAK: Is there anyone here who knows me? I am the Grand Duke.

THE FAT PRINCE: What is he?

THE SECOND IRONSHIRT: The Grand Duke. He really does know him.

THE FAT PRINCE: Good.

THE FIRST IRONSHIRT: Get on with the proceedings.

AZDAK: Listen! I'm accused of war-mongering. Ridiculous! Am saying: ridiculous! Is that enough? If not, have brought lawyers along. About 500. *He points behind him, pretending to be surrounded by lawyers.* Requisition all available seats for lawyers. *The Ironshirts laugh; the fat prince joins in.*

THE NEPHEW *to the Ironshirts:* Do you want me to try this case? I must admit I find it rather unusual. From the point of view of taste, I mean.

THE FIRST IRONSHIRT: Go on.

THE FAT PRINCE *smiling:* Let him have it, little fox!

THE NEPHEW: All right. People of Grusinia versus Grand Duke. What have you to say, defendant?

AZDAK: Any amount. Of course, have myself read war lost. Started war at the time on advice of patriots like Uncle

Kazbeki. Demand Uncle Kazbeki as witness. *The Ironshirts laugh.*

THE FAT PRINCE *to the Ironshirts, affably:* Quite a card, eh?

THE NEPHEW: Motion overruled. You're being accused not of declaring war, which every ruler has to do once in a while, but of conducting it badly.

AZDAK: Rot! Didn't conduct it at all! Had it conducted. Had it conducted by Princes. Made a mess of it, of course.

THE NEPHEW: Do you deny having been Commander in Chief?

AZDAK: Not at all. Always was Commander in Chief. Even at birth ticked off wet-nurse; dismissed turds promptly in potty. Got used to command. Always commanded officials to rob my cash-box. Officers flog soldiers only on my command. Landlords sleep with peasant's wives only when strictly commanded by me. Uncle Kazbeki here grew stomach only on my command.

THE IRONSHIRTS *clapping:* He's good! Up the Grand Duke!

THE FAT PRINCE: Answer him, little fox! I'm with you!

THE NEPHEW: I shall answer him according to the dignity of the law. Defendant, preserve the dignity of the law.

AZDAK: Agreed. Command you proceed with the trial.

THE NEPHEW: It's not your business to command me. So you claim the Princes forced you to declare war. Then how can you claim they made a mess of it?

AZDAK: Didn't send enough troops. Embezzled funds. Brought sick horses. During attack found drunk in whorehouse. Propose Uncle Kaz as witness. *The Ironshirts laugh.*

THE NEPHEW: Are you making the outrageous claim that the Princes of this country did not fight?

AZDAK: No. Princes fought. Fought for war contracts.

THE FAT PRINCE *jumping up:* That's too much! This man talks like a carpet weaver!

AZDAK: Really? Only telling the truth!

THE FAT PRINCE: Hang him! Hang him!

THE FIRST IRONSHIRT: Keep quiet. Get on, Excellency.

THE NEPHEW: Quiet! Now pass sentence. Must be hanged.

Hanged by the neck. Having lost war. Sentence passed. No appeal.

THE FAT PRINCE *hysterically:* Away with him! Away with him! Away with him!

AZDAK: Young man, seriously advise not to fall publicly into jerky, clipped manner of speech. Can't be employed as watchdog if howl like wolf. Got it?

THE FAT PRINCE: Hang him!

AZDAK: If people realize Princes talk same language as Grand Dukes, may even hang Grand Dukes and Princes. By the way, sentence quashed. Reason: war lost, but not for Princes. Princes have won *their* war. Got themselves paid 3,863,000 piastres for horses not delivered.

THE FAT PRINCE: Hang him!

AZDAK: 8,240,000 piastres for food supplies not produced.

THE FAT PRINCE: Hang him!

AZDAK: Are therefore victors. War lost only for Grusinia, which is not present in this Court.

THE FAT PRINCE: I think that's enough, my friends. *To Azdak:* You can withdraw, gaol-bird. *To the Ironshirts:* I think you can now ratify the new Judge's appointment, my friends.

THE FIRST IRONSHIRT: Yes, we can do that. Take down the Judge's robe. *One of the Ironshirts climbs on the back of another and pulls the robe off the hanged man.* And now—to the nephew— you be off so that we can put the right arse on the right seat. *To Azdak:* Step forward, you, and sit on the Judge's seat. *Azdak hesitates.* Sit down up there, man. *Azdak is thrust on to the seat by the Ironshirts.* The Judge was always a rascal. Now the rascal shall be the Judge. *The Judge's robe is placed round his shoulders, the wicker from a bottle on his head.* Look! There's a Judge for you!

THE SINGER

Now there was civil war in the land. The rulers were unsafe.

Now Azdak was made a Judge by the Ironshirts.

Now Azdak remained a Judge for two years.

THE SINGER WITH HIS MUSICIANS
> Great houses turn to ashes
>> And blood runs down the street.
> Rats come out of the sewers
>> And maggots out of the meat.
> The thug and the blasphemer
>> Lounge by the altar-stone:
> Now, now, now Azdak
>> Sits on the Judgment throne.

Azdak sits on the Judge's seat peeling an apple. Shauwa sweeps out the hall. On one side an invalid in a wheelchair, the accused doctor and a man in rags with a limp; opposite, a young man accused of blackmail. An Ironshirt stands on guard holding the Ironshirts' banner.

AZDAK: In view of the large number of cases, the Court today will hear two cases simultaneously. Before I open the proceedings, a short announcement: I receive—*he stretches out his hand; only the blackmailer produces some money and hands it to him*—I reserve for myself the right to punish one of these parties here—*he glances at the invalid*—for contempt of court. You—*to the doctor*—are a doctor, and you—*to the invalid*—are bringing a complaint against him. Is the doctor responsible for your condition?

THE INVALID: Yes. I had a stroke because of him.

AZDAK: That sounds like professional negligence.

THE INVALID: More than negligence. I gave this man money to study. So far he hasn't paid me back one penny. And when I heard he was treating a patient free, I had a stroke.

AZDAK: Rightly. *To the limping man.* And you, what do you want here?

THE LIMPING MAN: I'm the patient, your Worship.

AZDAK: He treated your leg?

THE LIMPING MAN: Not the right one. My rheumatism was in the left leg, and he operated on my right. That's why I'm limping now.

AZDAK: And you got that free?

THE INVALID: A 500-piastre operation free! For nothing! For a God-Bless-You! And I paid this man's studies! *To the doctor:* Did you learn to operate for nothing at school?

THE DOCTOR *to Azdak:* Your Worship, it is actually the custom to demand the fee before the operation, as the patient is more willing to pay before an operation than after. Which is only human. In this case I was convinced, when I started the operation, that my servant had already received the fee. In this I was mistaken.

THE INVALID: He was mistaken! A good doctor doesn't make mistakes. He examines before he operates.

AZDAK: That's right. *To Shauva:* Public Prosecutor, what's the other case about?

SHAUVA *busily sweeping:* Blackmail.

THE BLACKMAILER: High Court of Justice, I'm innocent. I only wanted to find out from the landowner in question if he really had raped his niece. He kindly informed me that this was not the case, and gave me the money only so that I could let my uncle study music.

AZDAK: Ah ha! *To the doctor:* You on the other hand can't produce any extenuating circumstances in your defence?

THE DOCTOR: Except that to err is human.

AZDAK: And you know that in money matters a good doctor is conscious of his responsibility? I once heard of a doctor who made a thousand piastres out of one sprained finger: he discovered it had something to do with the circulation of the blood, which a less good doctor would have overlooked. On another occasion, by careful treatment, he turned a mediocre gall bladder into a gold mine. You have no excuse, Doctor. The corn merchant Uxu made his son study medicine to get some knowledge of trade—our medical schools are that good. *To the blackmailer:* What's the name of the landowner?

SHAUVA: He doesn't want it to be known.

AZDAK: In that case I will pass judgment. The Court considers the blackmail proved. And you—*to the invalid*—are sentenced to a fine of 1000 piastres. If you get a second stroke the doctor will have to treat you free and if necessary amputate. *To the limping man:* As compensation, you will receive a bottle of embrocation. *To the blackmailer:* You are sentenced to hand over half the proceeds of your deal to the Public Prosecutor, to keep the landowner's name secret. You are advised, moreover, to study medicine. You seem well suited to that profession. And you, Doctor, are acquitted because of an inexcusable professional mistake. The next cases!

THE SINGER WITH HIS MUSICIANS
> Beware of willing Judges
>> For Truth is a black cat
> In a windowless room at midnight
>> And Justice a blind bat.
> A third and shrugging party
>> Alone can right our wrong.
> This, this, this, Azdak
>> Does for a mere song.

Enter Azdak from the caravansary on the highway, followed by the old, bearded innkeeper. The Judge's seat is carried by a manservant and Shauva. An Ironshirt with a banner takes up position.

AZDAK: Put it here. Then at least we can get some air and a little breeze from the lemon grove over there. It's good for Justice to do it in the open. The wind blows her skirts up and you can see what's underneath. Shauva, we have eaten too much. These rounds of inspection are very exhausting. *To the innkeeper:* So it's about your daughter-in-law?

THE INNKEEPER: Your Worship, it's about the family honour. I wish to bring an action on behalf of my son, who's gone on business across the mountain. This is the offending stableman, and here's my unfortunate daughter-in-law.
Enter the daughter-in-law, a voluptuous wench. She is veiled.

AZDAK *sitting down:* I receive. *Sighing, the innkeeper hands him some money.* Good. Now the formalities are disposed of. This is a case of rape?

THE INNKEEPER: Your Worship, I surprised this rascal in the stable in the act of laying our Ludovica in the straw.

AZDAK: Quite right, the stable. Beautiful horses. I particularly like the little roan.

THE INNKEEPER: The first thing I did of course was to berate Ludovica on behalf of my son.

AZDAK *seriously:* I said I liked the little roan.

THE INNKEEPER *coldly:* Really?—Ludovica admitted that the stableman took her against her will.

AZDAK: Take off your veil, Ludovica. *She does so.* Ludovica, you please the Court. Tell us how it happened.

LUDOVICA *as though well rehearsed:* When I entered the stable to look at the new foal, the stableman said to me of his own accord: 'It's hot today' and laid his hand on my left breast. I said to him: 'Don't do that!' But he continued to handle me indecently, which provoked my anger. Before I realized his sinful intentions, he became intimate with me. It had already happened when my father-in-law entered and accidentally trod on me.

THE INNKEEPER *explaining:* On behalf of my son.

AZDAK *to the stableman:* Do you admit that you started it?

THE STABLEMAN: Yes.

AZDAK: Ludovica, do you like to eat sweet things?

LUDOVICA: Yes, sunflower seeds.

AZDAK: Do you like sitting a long time in the tub?

LUDOVICA: Half an hour or so.

AZDAK: Public Prosecutor, just drop your knife on the floor. *Shauva does so.* Ludovica, go and pick up the Public Prosecutor's knife.

Ludovica, hips swaying, goes and picks up the knife.

Azdak points at her. Do you see that? The way it sways? The criminal element has been discovered. The rape has been proved. By eating too much, especially sweet things, by lying too long in warm water, by laziness and too soft a skin, you have raped the poor man. Do you imagine you can go around with a bottom like that and get away with it in Court? This is a case of deliberate assault with a dangerous weapon. You are sentenced to hand over to the Court the little roan which your father liked to ride on behalf of

his son. And now, Ludovica, come with me to the stable
so that the Court may investigage the scene of the crime.

*Azdak is carried on his Judge's seat by Ironshirts from place to
place on the Grusinian highway. Behind him come Shauwa dragging
the gallows and the stableman leading the little roan.*

THE SINGER WITH HIS MUSICIANS
No more did the Lower Orders
    Tremble in their shoes
At the bellows of their Betters
    At *Come-Here*'s and *Listen-You*'s.
His balances were crooked
    But they shouted in the streets:—
'Good, good, good is Azdak
    And the measure that he metes!'

He took them from Wealthy Peter
    To give to Penniless Paul
Sealed his illegal judgments
    With a waxen tear, and all
The rag-tag-and-bobtail
    Ran crying up and down:—
'Cheer, cheer, cheer for Azdak
    The darling of the town!'

The little group slowly withdraws.

To love your next-door neighbour
    Approach him with an axe
For prayers and saws and sermons
    Are unconvincing facts.
What miracles of preaching
    A good sharp blade can do:
So, so, so, so Azdak
    Makes miracles come true.

*Azdak's Judge's seat is in a tavern. Three farmers stand before
Azdak. Shauwa brings him wine. In a corner stands an old peasant
woman. In the open doorway, and outside, stand villagers and
spectators. An Ironshirt stands guard with a banner.*

AZDAK: The Public Prosecutor opens the proceedings.

SHAUVA: It's about a cow. For five weeks the defendant has had a cow in her stable, the property of farmer Suru. She was also found to be in the possession of a stolen ham. And cows belonging to farmer Shutoff were killed after he had asked the defendant to pay the rent for a field.

THE FARMERS: It's about my ham, Your Worship.—It's about my cow, Your Worship.—It's about my field, Your Worship.

AZDAK: Granny, what have you got to say to all this?

THE OLD WOMAN: Your Worship, one night towards morning, five weeks ago, there was a knock at my door, and outside stood a bearded man with a cow. He said, 'Dear woman, I am the miracle-working St Banditus. And because your son has been killed in the war, I bring you this cow as a keepsake. Take good care of it!'

THE FARMERS: The robber Irakli, Your Worship!—Her brother-in-law, Your Worship! The cattle thief, the incendiary!—He must be beheaded!

Outside a woman screams. The crowd grows restless and retreats. Enter the bandit Irakli, with a huge axe.

THE FARMERS: Irakli! *They cross themselves.*

THE BANDIT: A very good evening, dear friends! A glass of wine!

AZDAK: Public Prosecutor, a jug of wine for the guest. And who are you?

THE BANDIT: I'm a wandering hermit, Your Worship. And thank you for the kind gift. *He empties the glass which Shauva has brought.* Same again!

AZDAK: I'm Azdak. *He gets up and bows. The bandit also bows.* The Court welcomes the stranger hermit. Go on with your story, Granny.

THE OLD WOMAN: Your Worship, that first night I didn't know that St Banditus could work miracles, it was only the cow. But one night a few days later the farmer's servants came to take the cow away from me. Then they turned round in front of my door and went off without the cow.

And on their heads sprouted bumps big as a fist. Then I knew that St Banditus had changed their hearts and turned them into friendly people.

The bandit roars with laughter.

THE FIRST FARMER: I know what changed them.

AZDAK: That's good. You can tell us later. Continue.

THE OLD WOMAN: Your Worship, the next one to become a good man was farmer Shutoff—a devil, as everyone knows. But St Banditus brought it about that Shutoff let me off paying the rent for the field.

THE SECOND FARMER: Because my cows were killed in the field.

The bandit laughs.

THE OLD WOMAN *answering Azdak's sign to continue:* And then one morning the ham came flying in at my window. It hit me in the small of the back. I've been lame ever since. Look, Your Worship. *She limps a few steps. The bandit laughs.* I ask Your Worship: when was a poor old body ever given a ham except by a miracle?

The bandit starts sobbing.

AZDAK *rising from his seat:* Granny, that's a question that strikes straight at the Court's heart. Be so kind as to sit down here.

Hesitating, the old woman sits on the Judge's seat. Azdak sits on the floor, glass in hand.

> Little mother, I almost called you Mother Grusinia, the woebegone
> The bereaved one, whose sons are in the war.
> Who is beaten with fists, but full of hope.
> Who weeps when she is given a cow
> And is surprised when she is not beaten.
> Little mother, pass merciful sentence on us, the damned!

He bellows to the farmers.

Admit that you don't believe in miracles, you atheists! Each of you is sentenced to pay 500 piastres! For your lack of faith. Get out!

The farmers creep out.

And you, little mother, and you—*to the bandit*—pious man, drink a jug of wine with the Public Prosecutor and Azdak!

THE SINGER WITH HIS MUSICIANS

> To feed the starving people
> He broke the laws like bread
> There on the seat of justice
> With the gallows over his head
> For more than seven hundred
> Days he calmed their wails
> Well, well, well, did Azdak
> Measure with false scales.
>
> Two summers and two winters
> A poor man judged the poor
> And on the wreck of justice
> He brought them safe to shore
> For he spoke in the mob language
> That the mob understands.
> I, I, I, cried Azdak
> Take bribes from empty hands.

THE SINGER

> Then the era of disorder was over, the Grand Duke returned
> The Governor's wife returned, a Judgment was held.
> Many people died, the suburbs burned anew, and fear seized Azdak.

Azdak's Judge's seat stands again in the Court of Justice. Azdak sits on the ground mending a shoe and talking to Shauva. Noises outside. Above a wall the fat prince's head is carried by on a lance.

AZDAK: Shauva, your days of slavery are numbered, perhaps even the minutes. For a long time I have held you on the iron curb of reason, and it has made your mouth bloody. I have lashed you with arguments founded on reason, and ill-treated you with logic. You are by nature a weak creature, and if one slyly throws you an argument, you have to devour it; you can't resist. By nature you are compelled to lick the hand of a superior being, but superior beings

can be very different. And now comes your liberation, and
you will soon be able to follow your inclinations, which are
low. You will be able to follow your unerring instinct,
which teaches you to plant your heavy boot on the faces of
men. Gone is the era of confusion and disorder, and the
great times which I found described in the Song of Chaos
have not yet come. Let us now sing that song together in
memory of those wonderful days. Sit down and don't
violate the music. Don't be afraid. It sounds all right. It has
a popular refrain.

He sings

> Sister, hide your face; brother, take your knife, the times
> are out of joint.
> The noblemen are full of complaints, the simple folk full
> of joy.
> The city says: let us drive the strong ones out of our midst.
> Storm the government buildings, destroy the lists of the
> serfs.
> Now the masters' noses are put to the grindstone. Those
> who never saw the day have emerged.
> The poor-boxes of ebony are broken, the precious sesame
> wood is used for beds.
> He who lacked bread now possesses barns; he who lived
> on the corn of charity, now measures it out himself.

SHAUVA: Oh, oh, oh, oh.

AZDAK:

> Where are you, General? Please, please, please, restore
> order.
> The son of the nobleman can no longer be recognized; the
> child of the mistress becomes the son of her slave.
> The councillors are taking shelter in the barn; he who
> was barely allowed to sleep on the wall now lolls in bed.
> He who once rowed a boat now owns ships; when their
> owner looks for them, they are no longer his.
> Five men are sent out by their master. They say: go
> yourself, we have arrived.

SHAUVA: Oh, oh, oh, oh.

AZDAK:

> Where are you, General? Please, please, please restore order!

Yes, so it might have been, if order had been much longer neglected. But now the Grand Duke, whose life I saved like a fool, has returned to the Capital. And the Persians have lent him an army to restore order. The outer town is already in flames. Go and get me the Big Book I like to sit on. *Shauva brings the book from the Judge's seat. Azdak opens it.* This is the Statute Book and I've always used it, as you can confirm.

SHAUVA: Yes, to sit on.

AZDAK: Now I'd better look and see what they can do to me, because I've always allowed the have-nots to get away with everything. And I'll have to pay for it dearly. I helped to put Poverty on to its rickety legs, so they'll hang me for drunkenness. I peeped into the rich man's pocket, which is considered bad taste. And I can't hide anywhere, for all the world knows me, since I have helped the world.

SHAUVA: Someone's coming!

AZDAK *in a panic walks trembling to the seat:* The game is up! But I'll give no man the pleasure of seeing human greatness. I'll beg on my knees for mercy. Spittle will slobber down my chin. The fear of death is upon me.

Enter Natella Abashvili, the Governor's wife, followed by the Adjutant and an Ironshirt.

THE GOVERNOR'S WIFE: What kind of man is that, Shalva?

AZDAK: A willing one, Your Excellency, a man ready to oblige.

THE ADJUTANT: Natella Abashvili, wife of the late Governor, has just returned and is looking for her three-year-old son, Michael. She has been informed that the child was abducted to the mountains by a former servant.

AZDAK: It will be brought back, Your Highness, at your service.

THE ADJUTANT: They say that the person in question is passing it off as her own child.

AZDAK: She will be beheaded, Your Highness, at your service.

THE ADJUTANT: That's all.

THE GOVERNOR'S WIFE *leaving:* I don't like that man.

AZDAK *following her to the door, and bowing:* Everything will be arranged, Your Highness, at your service.

6

THE CHALK CIRCLE

THE SINGER

Now listen to the story of the trial concerning the child of
    the Governor Abashvili
To establish the true mother
By the famous test of the Chalk Circle.

*The courtyard of the lawcourts in Nukha. Ironshirts lead Michael
in, then go across the stage and out at the back. One Ironshirt holds
Grusha back under the doorway with his lance until the child has
been taken away. Then she is admitted. She is accompanied by the
former Governor's cook. Distant noises and a fire-red sky.*

GRUSHA: He's so good, he can wash himself already.

THE COOK: You're lucky. This is not a real Judge; this is
Azdak. He's a drunk and doesn't understand anything. And
the biggest thieves have been acquitted by him, because he
mixes everything up and because the rich never offer him
big enough bribes. The likes of us get off lightly sometimes.

GRUSHA: I need some luck today.

THE COOK: Touch wood. *She crosses herself.* I think I'd better
say a quick prayer that the Judge will be drunk.

*Her lips move in prayer, while Grusha looks round in vain for the
child.*

THE COOK: What I can't understand is why you want to hold
on to it at any price, if it's not yours. In these days.

GRUSHA: It's mine, I've brought it up.

THE COOK: But didn't you ever wonder what would happen when she returned?

GRUSHA: At first I thought I'd give it back to her. Then I thought she wouldn't return.

THE COOK: And a borrowed coat keeps one warm, too, eh? *Grusha nods.* I'll swear anything you like, because you're a decent person. *Memorizes aloud:* I had him in my care for five piastres, and on Thursday evening, when the riots started, Grusha came to fetch him. *She sees the soldier, Chachava, approaching.* But you have done Simon great wrong. I've talked to him. He can't understand it.

GRUSHA *unaware of Simon's presence:* I can't be bothered with that man just now, if he doesn't understand anything.

THE COOK: He has understood that the child is not yours; but that you're married and won't be free until death parts you —he can't understand that.

Grusha sees Simon and greets him.

SIMON *gloomily:* I wanted to tell the woman that I am ready to swear I am the father of the child.

GRUSHA *low:* That's right, Simon.

SIMON: At the same time, I would like to say that I am hereby not bound to anything; nor the woman, either.

THE COOK: That's unnecessary. She's married. You know that.

SIMON: That's her business and doesn't need rubbing in.

Enter two Ironshirts.

THE IRONSHIRTS: Where's the Judge?—Has anyone seen the Judge?

GRUSHA *who has turned away and covered her face:* Stand in front of me. I shouldn't have come to Nukha. If I run into the Ironshirt, the one I hit over the head . . .

The Ironshirt who has brought in the child steps forward.

THE IRONSHIRT: The Judge isn't here.

The two Ironshirts go on searching.

THE COOK: I hope something hasn't happened to him. With any other Judge you'd have less chance than a chicken has teeth.

Enter another Ironshirt.

THE IRONSHIRT *who had inquired for the Judge, to the other Ironshirt:* There are only two old people and a child here. The Judge has bolted.

THE OTHER IRONSHIRT: Go on searching!

The first two Ironshirts exit quickly. The third remains behind. Grusha lets out a scream. The Ironshirt turns round. He is the Corporal, and has a large scar right across his face.

THE IRONSHIRT *in the gateway:* What's the matter, Shotta? Do you know her?

THE CORPORAL *after a long stare:* No.

THE IRONSHIRT: She's the one who's supposed to have stolen the Abashvili child. If you know anything about it, Shotta, you can make a packet of money.

Exit the Corporal, cursing.

THE COOK: Was it him? *Grusha nods.* I think he'll keep his mouth shut, otherwise he'll have to admit he was after the child.

GRUSHA *relieved:* I'd almost forgotten I'd saved the child from them . . .

Enter the Governor's wife, followed by the Adjutant and two lawyers.

THE GOVERNOR'S WIFE: Thank God! At least the common people aren't here. I can't stand their smell, it always gives me migraine.

THE FIRST LAWYER: Madam, I must ask you to be as careful as possible in everything you say, until we have another Judge.

THE GOVERNOR'S WIFE: But I didn't say anything, Illo Shuboladze. 1 love the people—with their simple, straightforward ways. It's just their smell that brings on my migraine.

THE SECOND LAWYER: There will hardly be any spectators. Most of the population is behind locked doors because of the riots in the outer town.

THE GOVERNOR'S WIFE *looking at Grusha:* Is that the creature?

THE FIRST LAWYER: I beg you, most gracious Natella

Abashvili, to abstain from all invective until it is absolutely certain that the Grand Duke has appointed a new Judge and we have got rid of the present one, who is about the lowest ever seen in a Judge's robe. And things seem to be on the move, as you will see.

Ironshirts enter the courtyard.

THE COOK: Her Ladyship wouldn't hesitate to pull your hair out if she didn't know that Azdak is for the poor people. He goes by the face.

Two Ironshirts begin by fastening a rope to the pillar. Azdak, in chains, is led in, followed by Shauwa, also in chains. The three farmers bring up the rear.

ONE IRONSHIRT: Trying to run away, eh? *He beats Azdak.*

ONE FARMER: Pull the Judge's robe off before we string him up!

Ironshirts and farmers pull the robe off Azdak. His torn underwear becomes visible. Then someone kicks him.

AN IRONSHIRT *pushing him on to someone else:* Anyone want a bundle of Justice? Here it is!

Accompanied by shouts of 'It's all yours!' and 'I don't want it!' they hurl Azdak back and forth until he collapses. Then he is hauled up and dragged under the noose.

THE GOVERNOR'S WIFE *who, during the 'ball-game', has been clapping her hands hysterically:* I disliked that man from the moment I first saw him.

AZDAK *covered in blood, panting:* I can't see. Give me a rag.

THE OTHER IRONSHIRT: What is it you want to see?

AZDAK: You, you dogs! *He wipes the blood out of his eyes with his shirt.* Good morning, dogs! How are you, dogs? How's the dog world? Does it stink good? Have you got another boot to lick? Are you back at each other's throats, dogs?

Enter a dust-covered rider accompanied by a corporal. He takes some documents from a leather case and looks through them. He interrupts.

THE RIDER: Stop! I bring a despatch from the Grand Duke, containing the latest appointments.

THE CORPORAL *bellows:* Atten - shun!
All jump to attention.

THE RIDER: Of the new Judge it says: We appoint a man whom we have to thank for the saving of a life of the utmost importance to the country. A certain Azdak in Nukha. Which is he?

SHAUVA *pointing:* That's him on the gallows, Your Excellency.

THE CORPORAL *bellowing:* What's going on here?

THE IRONSHIRT: I ask to be allowed to report that His Worship has already been His Worship. He was declared the enemy of the Grand Duke only on these farmers' denunciation.

THE CORPORAL *pointing at the farmers:* March them off! *They are marched off, bowing incessantly.* See to it that His Worship is exposed to no more indignities.
Exit the rider with the corporal.

THE COOK *to Shauva:* She clapped her hands! I hope he saw it!

THE FIRST LAWYER: This is a catastrophe.
Azdak has fainted. Coming to, he is dressed again in a Judge's robe. He walks away, swaying, from the group of Ironshirts.

THE IRONSHIRTS: Don't take it amiss, Your Worship. What are Your Worship's wishes?

AZDAK: Nothing, fellow dogs. An occasional boot to lick. *To Shauva:* I pardon you. *He is unchained.* Fetch me some of the red wine. The sweetest. *Exit Shauva.* Get out of here, I've got to judge a case. *The Ironshirts go. Shauva returns with a jug of wine. Azdak takes deep gulps.* Get me something for my backside. *Shauva brings the Statute Book and puts it on the Judge's seat. Azdak sits on it.* I receive! *The faces of the prosecutors, among whom a worried council has been held, show smiles of relief. They whisper.*

THE COOK: Oh dear!

SIMON: 'A well can't be filled with dew!' they say.

THE LAWYERS *approaching Azdak, who stands up expectantly:* An absolutely ridiculous case, Your Worship. The accused has abducted the child and refuses to hand it over.

AZDAK *stretching out his hand, and glancing at Grusha:* A most attractive person. *He receives more money.* I open the proceedings and demand the absolute truth. *To Grusha:* Especially from you.

THE FIRST LAWYER: High Court of Justice! Blood, as the saying goes, is thicker than water. This old proverb . . .

AZDAK: The Court wants to know the lawyer's fee.

THE FIRST LAWYER *surprised:* I beg your pardon? *Azdak rubs his thumb and index finger.* Oh, I see. 500 piastres, Your Worship, is the answer to the Court's somewhat unusual question.

AZDAK: Did you hear? The question is unusual. I ask it because I listen to you in a quite different way if I know you are good.

THE FIRST LAWYER *bowing:* Thank you, Your Worship. High Court of Justice! Of all bonds the bonds of blood are the strongest. Mother and child—is there a more intimate relationship? Can one tear a child from its mother? High Court of Justice! She has conceived it in the holy ecstasies of love. She has carried it in her womb. She has fed it with her blood. She has borne it with pain. High Court of Justice! It has been observed, Your Worship, how even the wild tigress, robbed of her young, roams restless through the mountains, reduced to a shadow. Nature herself . . .

AZDAK *interrupting, to Grusha:* What's your answer to all this and anything else the lawyer might have to say?

GRUSHA: He's mine.

AZDAK: Is that all? I hope you can prove it. In any case, I advise you to tell me why you think the child should be given to you.

GRUSHA: I've brought him up according to my best knowledge and conscience. I always found him something to eat. Most of the time he had a roof over his head. And I went to all sorts of trouble for him. I had expenses, too. I didn't think of my own comfort. I brought up the child to be friendly with everyone. And from the beginning I taught him to work as well as he could. But he's still very small.

THE FIRST LAWYER: Your Worship, it is significant that the person herself doesn't claim any bond of blood between herself and this child.

AZDAK: The Court takes note.

THE FIRST LAWYER: Thank you, Your Worship. Please permit a woman who has suffered much—who has already lost her husband and now also has to fear the loss of her child—to address a few words to you. Her Highness, Natella Abashvili . . .

THE GOVERNOR'S WIFE *quietly:* A most cruel fate, sir, forces me to ask you to return my beloved child. It's not for me to describe to you the tortures of a bereaved mother's soul, the anxiety, the sleepless nights, the . . .

THE SECOND LAWYER *exploding:* It's outrageous the way this woman is treated. She's not allowed to enter her husband's palace. The revenue of her estates is blocked. She is told cold-bloodedly that it's tied to the heir. She can't do anything without the child. She can't even pay her lawyers. *To the first lawyer who, desperate about this outburst, makes frantic gestures to stop him speaking:* Dear Illo Shuboladze, why shouldn't it be divulged now that it's the Abashvili estates that are at stake?

THE FIRST LAWYER: Please, Honoured Sandro Oboladze! We had agreed . . . *To Azdak:* Of course it is correct that the trial will also decide whether our noble client will obtain the right to dispose of the large Abashvili estates. I say 'also' on purpose, because in the foreground stands the human tragedy of a mother, as Natella Abashvili has rightly explained at the beginning of her moving statement. Even if Michael Abashvili were *not* the heir to the estates, he would still be the dearly beloved child of my client.

AZDAK: Stop! The Court is touched by the mention of the estates. It's a proof of human feeling.

THE SECOND LAWYER: Thanks, Your Worship. Dear Illo Shuboladze, in any case we can prove that the person who took possession of the child is not the child's mother. Permit me to lay before the Court the bare facts. By an unfortunate chain of circumstances, the child, Michael Abashvili, was left behind while his mother was making her escape. Grusha, the Palace kitchenmaid, was present on this Easter Sunday and was observed busying herself with the child . . .

THE COOK: All her mistress was thinking about was what kind of dresses she would take along.

THE SECOND LAWYER *unmoved:* Almost a year later Grusha turned up in a mountain village with a child, and there entered into matrimony with . . .

AZDAK: How did you get into that mountain village?

GRUSHA: On foot, Your Worship. And he was mine.

SIMON: I am the father, Your Worship.

THE COOK: I had him in my care for five piastres, Your Worship.

THE SECOND LAWYER: This man is engaged to Grusha, High Court of Justice, and for this reason his testimony is not reliable.

AZDAK: Are you the man she married in the mountain village?

SIMON: No, Your Worship, she married a peasant.

AZDAK *winking at Grusha:* Why? *Pointing at Simon:* Isn't he any good in bed? Tell the truth.

GRUSHA: We didn't get that far. I married because of the child, so that he should have a roof over his head. *Pointing at Simon.* He was in the war, Your Worship.

AZDAK: And now he wants you again, eh?

SIMON: I want to state in evidence . . .

GRUSHA *angrily:* I am no longer free, Your Worship.

AZDAK: And the child, you claim, is the result of whoring? *Grusha does not answer.* I'm going to ask you a question: What kind of child is it? Is it one of those ragged streeturchins? Or is it a child from a well-to-do family?

GRUSHA *angrily:* It's an ordinary child.

AZDAK: I mean, did he have fine features from the beginning?

GRUSHA: He had a nose in his face.

AZDAK: He had a nose in his face. I consider that answer of yours to be important. They say of me that once, before passing judgment, I went out and sniffed at a rosebush. Tricks of this kind are necessary nowadays. I'll cut things short now, and listen no longer to your lies. *To Grusha:* Especially yours. *To the group of defendants:* I can imagine what you've cooked up between you to cheat me. I know you. You're swindlers.

GRUSHA *suddenly:* I can quite understand your wanting to cut it short, having seen what you received!

AZDAK: Shut up! Did I receive anything from you?

GRUSHA *while the cook tries to restrain her:* Because I haven't got anything.

AZDAK: Quite true. I never get a thing from starvelings. I might just as well starve myself. You want justice, but do you want to pay for it? When you go to the butcher you know you have to pay. But to the Judge you go as though to a funeral supper.

SIMON *loudly:* 'When the horse was shod, the horsefly stretched out its leg', as the saying is.

AZDAK *eagerly accepting the challenge:* 'Better a treasure in the sewer than a stone in the mountain stream.'

SIMON: ' "A fine day. Let's go fishing," said the angler to the worm.'

AZDAK: ' "I'm my own master," said the servant, and cut off his foot.'

SIMON: ' "I love you like a father," said the Czar to the peasant, and had the Czarevitch's head chopped off.'

AZDAK: 'The fool's worst enemy is himself.'

SIMON: But 'a fart has no nose'.

AZDAK: Fined ten piastres for indecent language in Court. That'll teach you what Justice is.

GRUSHA: That's a fine kind of Justice. You jump on us because we don't talk so refined as that lot with their lawyers.

AZDAK: Exactly. The likes of you are too stupid. It's only right that you should get it in the neck.

GRUSHA: Because you want to pass the child on to her. She who is too refined even to know how to change its nappies! You don't know any more about Justice than I do, that's clear.

AZDAK: There's something in that. I'm an ignorant man. I haven't even a decent pair of trousers under my robe. See for yourself. With me, everything goes on food and drink. I was educated in a convent school. Come to think of it, I'll fine you ten piastres, too. For contempt of Court. What's more, you're a very silly girl to turn me against you, instead of making eyes at me and wagging your backside a bit to keep me in a good temper. Twenty piastres!

GRUSHA: Even if it were thirty, I'd tell you what I think of your justice, you drunken onion! How dare you talk to me as though you were the cracked Isaiah on the church window! When they pulled you out of your mother, it wasn't planned that you'd rap her over the knuckles for pinching a little bowl of corn from somewhere! Aren't you ashamed of yourself when you see how afraid I am of you? But you've let yourself become their servant. So that their houses are not taken away, because they've stolen them. Since when do houses belong to bed-bugs? But you're on the look-out, otherwise they couldn't drag our men into their wars. You bribe-taker!

Azdak gets up. He begins to beam. With a little hammer he knocks on the table half-heartedly as if to get silence. But as Grusha's scolding continues, he only beats time with it.

I've no respect for you. No more than for a thief or a murderer with a knife, who does what he wants. You can take the child away from me, a hundred against one, but I tell you one thing: for a profession like yours, they ought to choose only bloodsuckers and men who rape children. As a punishment. To make them sit in judgment over their fellow men, which is worse than swinging from the gallows.

AZDAK *sitting down:* Now it will be thirty! And I won't go on brawling with you as though we were in a tavern. What would happen to my dignity as a Judge? I've lost all interest

in your case. Where's the couple who wanted a divorce?
To Shauva: Bring them in. This case is adjourned for fifteen
minutes.

THE FIRST LAWYER *to the Governor's wife:* Without producing
any more evidence, Madam, we have the verdict in the bag.

THE COOK *to Grusha:* You've gone and spoiled your chances
with him. You won't get the child now.
Enter a very old couple.

THE GOVERNOR'S WIFE: Shalva, my smelling salts!

AZDAK: I receive. *The old couple do not understand.* I hear you
want to be divorced. How long have you been living
together?

THE OLD WOMAN: Forty years, Your Worship.

AZDAK: And why d'you want a divorce?

THE OLD MAN: We don't like each other, Your Worship.

AZDAK: Since when?

THE OLD WOMAN: Oh, from the very beginning, Your
Worship.

AZDAK: I'll consider your case and deliver my verdict when
I'm finished with the other one. *Shauva leads them into the
background.* I need the child. *He beckons Grusha towards him
and bends not unkindly towards her.* I've noticed that you have a
soft spot for justice. I don't believe he's your child, but if
he were yours, woman, wouldn't you want him to be rich?
You'd only have to say he isn't yours and at once he'd have
a palace, scores of horses in his stable, scores of beggars on
his doorstep, scores of soldiers in his service, and scores of
petitioners in his courtyard. Now, what d'you say? Don't
you want him to be rich?
Grusha is silent.

THE SINGER: Listen now to what the angry girl thought, but
didn't say. *He sings:*

He who wears the shoes of gold
Tramples on the weak and old
Does evil all day long
And mocks at wrong.

> O to carry as one's own
> Heavy is the heart of stone.
> The power to do ill
> Wears out the will.
>
> Hunger he will dread
> Not those who go unfed:
> Fear the fall of night
> But not the light.

AZDAK: I think I understand you, woman.

GRUSHA: I won't give him away. I've brought him up, and he knows me.

Enter Shauva with the child.

THE GOVERNOR'S WIFE: It's in rags!

GRUSHA: That's not true. I wasn't given the time to put on his good shirt.

THE GOVERNOR'S WIFE: It's been in a pig-sty.

GRUSHA *furious:* I'm no pig, but there are others who are. Where did you leave your child?

THE GOVERNOR'S WIFE: I'll let you have it, you vulgar person. *She is about to throw herself on Grusha, but is restrained by her lawyers.* She's a criminal! She must be flogged! Right away!

THE SECOND LAWYER *holding his hand over her mouth:* Most gracious Natella Abashvili, you promised . . . Your Worship, the plaintiff's nerves . . .

AZDAK: Plaintiff and defendant! The Court has listened to your case, and has come to no decision as to who the real mother of this child is. I as Judge have the duty of choosing a mother for the child. I'll make a test. Shauva, get a piece of chalk and draw a circle on the floor. *Shauva does so.* Now place the child in the centre. *Shauva puts Michael, who smiles at Grusha, in the centre of the circle.* Plaintiff and defendant, stand near the circle, both of you. *The Governor's wife and Grusha step up to the circle.* Now each of you take the child by a hand. The true mother is she who has the strength to pull the child out of the circle, towards herself.

THE SECOND LAWYER *quickly:* High Court of Justice, I protest! I object that the fate of the great Abashvili estates, which are bound up with the child as the heir, should be made dependent on such a doubtful wrestling match. Moreover, my client does not command the same physical strength as this person, who is accustomed to physical work.

AZDAK: She looks pretty well fed to me. Pull!

The Governor's wife pulls the child out of the circle to her side. Grusha has let it go and stands aghast.

THE FIRST LAWYER *congratulating the Governor's wife:* What did I say! The bonds of blood!

AZDAK *to Grusha:* What's the matter with you? You didn't pull!

GRUSHA: I didn't hold on to him. *She runs to Azdak.* Your Worship, I take back everything I said against you. I ask your forgiveness. If I could just keep him until he can speak properly. He knows only a few words.

AZDAK: Don't influence the Court! I bet you know only twenty yourself. All right, I'll do the test once more, to make certain.

The two women take up positions again.

AZDAK: Pull!

Again Grusha lets go of the child.

GRUSHA *in despair:* I've brought him up! Am I to tear him to pieces? I can't do it!

AZDAK *rising:* And in this manner the Court has established the true mother. *To Grusha:* Take your child and be off with it. I advise you not to stay in town with him. *To the Governor's wife:* And you disappear before I fine you for fraud. Your estates fall to the city. A playground for children will be made out of them. They need one, and I have decided it shall be called after me—The Garden of Azdak.

The Governor's wife has fainted and is carried out by the Adjutant. Her lawyers have preceded her. Grusha stands motionless. Shauwa leads the child towards her.

AZDAK: Now I'll take off this Judge's robe—it has become

too hot for me. I'm not cut out for a hero. But I invite you all to a little farewell dance, outside on the meadow. Oh, I had almost forgotten something in my excitement. I haven't signed the decree for divorce.

Using the Judge's seat as a table, he writes something on a piece of paper and prepares to leave. Dance music has started.

SHAUVA *having read what is on the paper:* But that's not right. You haven't divorced the old couple. You've divorced Grusha from her husband.

AZDAK: Have I divorced the wrong ones? I'm sorry, but it'll have to stand. I never retract anything. If I did, there'd be no law and order. *To the old couple:* Instead, I'll invite you to my feast. You won't mind dancing with each other. *To Grusha and Simon:* I've still got 40 piastres coming from you.

SIMON *pulling out his purse:* That's cheap, Your Worship. And many thanks.

AZDAK *pocketing the money:* I'll need it.

GRUSHA: So we'd better leave town tonight, eh, Michael? *About to take the child on her back. To Simon:* You like him?

SIMON *taking the child on his back:* With my respects, I like him.

GRUSHA: And now I can tell you: I took him because on that Easter Sunday I got engaged to you. And so it is a child of love. Michael, let's dance.

She dances with Michael. Simon dances with the cook. The old couple dance with each other. Azdak stands lost in thought. The dancers soon hide him from view. Occasionally he is seen again, but less and less as more couples enter and join the dance.

THE SINGER

    And after this evening Azdak disappeared and was never seen again.

    But the people of Grusinia did not forget him and often remembered

    His time of Judgment as a brief

    Golden Age that was almost just.

The dancing couples dance out. Azdak has disappeared.

But you, who have listened to the story of the Chalk
    Circle
Take note of the meaning of the ancient song:
That what there is shall belong to those who are good for
    it, thus
The children to the maternal, that they thrive;
The carriages to good drivers, that they are driven well;
And the valley to the waterers, that it shall bear fruit.

Notes

Scene 1

3 *Caucasian village* — the Caucasus is a range of mountains lying between the Black Sea and the Caspian Sea, covering an area historically fought over by Russia, Turkey and Iran. On its southern slopes lies the province of Georgia, which was occupied by the Red Army in 1921 and became a republic within the Soviet Union. Stalin was a Georgian. In World War II the Caucasus was the scene of heavy fighting from 1942 until the Germans were driven out in 1944.

3 *kolchos* — collective farm. Between 1929 and 1938 under Stalin land was taken out of the hands of individual peasants and merged into large holdings which could be worked collectively on a large scale. The system has not yet been able to feed the Russian people efficiently.

3 *A Girl Tractor Driver* — the tractor driver who represents the mechanisation and modernisation of agriculture under Communism is something of a stock figure in Soviet-inspired works of Socialist Realism. That the driver is a girl here indicates the important role of women in building the new society.

3 *I set fire to it* — setting fire to all usable plant, buildings and crops ahead of the advancing Germans was a military tactic known as the scorched earth policy.

3 *Nukha* — an ancient city on the southern slopes of the Caucasus in eastern Georgia.

3 *Rosa Luxemburg* — (1870-1919) a German socialist of Polish extraction who was instrumental in founding the German Communist Party. She was murdered by right-wing para-militaries of the *Freikorps* in 1919. In 1934 a delegation of German writers visited a wine collective named after her near Tbilisi. They commented favourably on the international workforce of Russians, Turks and Germans, and on an ambitious irrigation scheme.

4 *enormous cheese wrapped in cloth* — Brecht, himself a cheese fan, wanted it to be unwrapped carefully and tasted seriously. Food, as Azdak later shows, is a serious matter. Here it has to be clear to the audience that the cheese is generally agreed to be good, hence the laughter when the Old Man claims otherwise.

4   *why does one love one's country* — the Expert makes it clear that there is room in the system not only for the rational approach which is about to be stressed, but also for emotional ties to the land.

5   *but to Prince Kazbeki* — this implies that the old man was released from feudal bondage by the Revolution in 1917. An ancestor of Prince Kazbeki appears in scenes 2 and 5 in the ancient Chinese play.

5   *According to the law* — this speech and the Girl Tractor Driver's response were inserted to emphasise the theme of social justice in 1956 at the time when *The Struggle for the Valley* was changed from the prologue into scene 1. The concept of a law based not on precedent, or on established codes, but on constant reassessment of social desirability links *The Struggle for the Valley* with the ancient play that follows.

5   *a piece of land as a tool* — the Expert gives an elementary lesson on the socialist view of land. Not only is it not private property, it is not even the hereditary right of any group, but a national asset from which the community expects a return. It should therefore go to whoever can put it to most productive use. That Soviet agriculture would prove inefficient is something Brecht did not foresee, or even recognize when he saw it.

6   *without ammunition for our few rifles* — the fruit-growers had taken to the hills as partisans during the German occupation (1942-44). The reminder that the irrigation plan was conceived during the resistance disposes even the goat-breeders favourably towards it, as the applause all round shows.

6   *Mayakovsky* — Vladimir Mayakovsky (1893-1930), a Russian born in Georgia, was a poet and dramatist of the Revolution who, like Brecht, was accused of formalism under Stalin. He committed suicide in 1930 and had not been rehabilitated when Brecht used this quotation.

7   *machines and projects* — the constructive optimism with which Brecht invests Georgia in 1944 echoes the revolutionary pathos of Soviet films like *Earth*. Recent appraisals of collectivisation such as Heiner Müller's *Peasants* (*Die Bauern*, 1964) show a bleaker version of the re-organisation of agriculture under socialism, albeit in post-war East Germany.

7   *Arkady Cheidze* — Brecht invented the name, though, intriguingly, there was a leading Georgian Social Democrat called Nicolai Semenovich Cheidze who was an early rival of Stalin and a

critic of Lenin.

8   *comes north more often* — this suggests that *The Struggle for the Valley* takes place in the northern mountains to which Grusha flees in scene 3.

8   *a play with songs* — what follows is a kind of *Singspiel* or ballad-opera, and Paul Dessau wrote 45 separate pieces of music for it.

8   *from the Chinese* — Brecht gives credit here to his source, a thirteenth-century Chinese play, *Hui Lan Chi* (*The Chalk Circle*) by Li Hsing Tao, which had been translated into German in the 1920s by Brecht's friend, Klabund.

8   *difficult debate* — it seems almost ironic to call the rather anodyne exchange of views that has taken place a difficult debate, but the Singer had not heard it anyway.

8   *old and new wisdom* — the old wisdom is the manner in which the Azdak resolves the conflict in *The Chalk Circle*, the new wisdom is the Soviet reason which has resolved the problem of the valley.

8   *Tiflis* — now Tbilisi, capital of Georgia.

8   *Couldn't you make it shorter* — this is more curt than the original version where the expert plaintively remarks that he has to get back to Tiflis and a young girl appeals on his behalf to Cheidze to cut it short. This play is a long one and it is as if Brecht were forestalling directors who would seek to cut it.

Scene 2

9   *The Singer* — the Singer functions as prompter, stage-manager, master of ceremonies and commentator. Whereas scene captions explained the historical background in *Mother Courage*, it is the Singer and the musicians who provide the epic commentary in *The Chalk Circle*. The singer outlines the action and the characters then illustrate it in *tableaux*.

9   *Once upon a time* — the Singer's ballad starts with the traditional fairy-tale formula and sets the scene for the Grusha episode long ago in the city of the damned with its rich, cruel governor and suffering population. The episode that follows demonstrates this. Miming of visuals to a commentary is characteristic of Japanese Bunraku and certain forms of Chinese theatre. The city in question is Nukha.

9   *Grusinia* — from the German *Grusinien*. Brecht uses this old form which derives from the Russian for Georgia — Gruziya.

10 *The Adjutant approaches the rider and stops him* — the rider comes from the front with, the Adjutant suspects, bad news. The Governor demonstrates his indifference to the war, and the Fat Prince betrays his concern that the messenger may give him away.

10 *new wing on the east side* — the Governor presses on with rebuilding his palace in spite of military reverses. The slum dwellings of his subjects are to be summarily demolished to make way for the new wing. Azdak will turn the Governor's estates into a children's playground at the end of the play.

11 *Niko Mikadze* — and Mikha Loladze, the rival paediatricians, are a comic double act, down to their very names.

12 *The city lies still* — the Singer provides continuity, telling the audience that the next two figures they are going to meet are a kitchen maid and a soldier. A bantering directness enters the dialogue when the lower-class figures appear. The tone is naive and flirtatious rather than earthy.

13 *Simon Chachava* — Grusha already knows his name, though this is the first time he has approached her.

13 *Not with another soldier!* — Brecht modulates the tone skilfully to show that the Soldier's intentions are serious, though his approach is playful.

13 *why are there armed men?* — the Singer's rhetorical questions complement the signs that pass between the Fat Prince and the Ironshirts, indicating economically that a palace revolution is afoot.

14 *Where was Brother Kazbeki?* — the Governor is suspicious of the discrepancy he has spotted in the Fat Prince's remarks, but he is too indolent to pursue the matter.

14 *not before the banquet* — this is the third time the Governor has refused to accept the rider's message, repetition making the significance of his non-speaking part clear.

15 *Chopped to pieces for the Governor* — dramatic irony, as the Ironshirt with the lance instantly proves.

15 *Oh, blindness of the great!* — there is an echo of Aeschylus as the Singer, like the chorus in Greek tragedy, pronounces moral judgement on the great. Brecht gives a Marxist twist to the baroque image of Fortune's wheel by making it the hope of the people — after the last revolution.

16 *share in their misfortunes* — the little people rarely share the good fortune — only the misfortunes — of the ruling classes. The divergent interests of the two classes which the Singer pinpoints here is a constant theme of Brecht's major plays, which sympathise with the oppressed class.

17   *How can stabbing harm the knife?* – by producing this piece of folk wisdom Simon Chachava proves that he is unconcerned about danger. It shows him to be an unimaginative soul, and it prepares us for his proverb contest with Azdak later in the play.

17   *The soldier is a pig-headed man* – Grusha notices that Simon cannot see where his own interest lies. She will soon prove prone to the same error herself. 'The young lady' and 'the soldier' address one another in the third person to avoid sentimentality in the proposal scene.

19   *In two weeks. Or three* – the separation turns out to be much longer. Simon's words echo the patriots on both sides in 1914 who set out for the front singing on the assumption that World War I would be over by Christmas.

19   *all is as it was* – having avoided sentiment in the previous dialogue, Brecht uses verse for Grusha's beautiful, comprehensive pledge. It is charged with dramatic irony since Grusha contracts (but does not consummate) a marriage in Simon's absence.

19   *harshly* – note the abrupt shifts of tone from one episode to the next.

20   *Why should they?* – the pause that follows shows that the servants can think of reasons, though her class arrogance blinds the Governor's Wife to her real situation.

21   *Quick! Quick!* – this final exchange with the adjutant becomes increasingly frantic as Natella toys with her wardrobe. Brecht is using the prolonged departure to create suspense.

22   *Deceitfully* – the stage direction shows that it has to be clear to the audience that Grusha is being put upon from the start.

23   *They'll slaughter whole families* – in a hereditary, dynastic society all possible pretenders have to be wiped out. The Czar's family were victims of this principle in Russia in 1917.

23   *stubbornly* – it is now Grusha's turn to ignore her own interests. There is an echo here of Kattrin in the officers' shirts scene in *Mother Courage* in the way Grusha gives in to her maternal instinct.

24   *As she was standing* – the Singer functions here as a kind of voice-over, rationalising, expanding, poeticising and commenting on Grusha's response to the situation.

25   *The light grown dimmer* – in general, Brecht maintained an even, bright, white level of lighting, in keeping with the anti-illusionistic aims of his theatre. Here the dimmer is used to indicate the passage of time and is not intended as symbolic or atmospheric.

25 *Terrible is the temptation to do good!* — this paradox indicates that Grusha's humane gesture is going to cause her much trouble. The explanation is a social one; in an inhuman, exploitative society altruism is always a risk.

Scene 3

25 *How will the merciful escape the merciless* — the Musicians join in and we have a two-part commentary. The Singer sketches the action, the Musicians, in the manner of the trailer at the end of a thirties Hollywood serial, whet the audience's appetite. Brecht called *The Flight into the Northern Mountains* a 'very epic' sequence, no doubt because it is built up of short 'station-scenes' between which Grusha moves on. J.M. Ritchie suggests that it was conceived as a chase sequence in the manner of the Western or gangster movie.

26 *Sosso Robakidse* — the patriotic ballad which Grusha sings to keep her spirits up tells of four unsuccessful Grusinian generals and the folk-hero Sosso Robakidse (whom Brecht invented), who takes over, galvanizes his troops and defeats the Iranians. It announces the theme of the effete, corrupt aristocracy which the Azdak story develops.

26 *A peasant's cottage appears* — in Brecht's own production the cottage travelled round to meet Grusha who was walking against the movement of the revolving stage.

26 *soldiers from the city* — the Ironshirts from Nukha have been plundering the countryside, causing shortages and forcing up prices.

28 *caravansary* — wayside inn or staging post for camel trains in the Middle East and Asia.

27 *Grusha dressed in the brocade coat* — Grusha is trying to pass herself off as an aristocrat.

28 *the pink is exquisite* — the Innkeeper's tasteful appreciation of nature masks a cut-throat businessman.

29 *needed it all that urgently* — the dash implies that this statement hides something, and the following dialogue suggests that the Elder Lady's husband had his throat cut and the Younger's was whipped. So they are in fact fugitives.

30 *Anastasia Katarinovska* — in an early version of the play Natella Abashvili was called Anastasia Abashvili, in which case it was clear that Grusha is posing as her former mistress in this scene. She even reveals Michael's name, a dangerous slip. It is confusing of Brecht not to have substituted Natella for Anastasia here.

30 *a look at your hands* — during the Russian Revolution, examination of the hands was a standard method of identifying non-proletarians; Brecht alluded to this in rehearsals of the play.

32 *Look before you leap* — the Servant, like Simon Chachava, has a predilection for proverbs. He is the first character to display class consciousness and solidarity with Grusha in her flight.

32 *a hollow reed or a tinkling cymbal* — the Corporal works a variation on the Biblical simile 'sounding brass or a tinkling cymbal' (I Corinthians 13:1). The Corporal is a loud-mouthed bully. He is chastising the private for being a pale reflection of a real soldier because he failed to enter into the spirit of a recent rape. This episode on the highway shows what Grusha is up against.

34 *You can't ask that of me, Michael* — Grusha has sized up the Peasant Woman and feels she is kind; she has milk and can provide for Michael, so Grusha can leave him with a clear conscience, aware as she still is that her own interests lie elsewhere.

35 *like one impoverished I'm going* — Grusha steps out of hiding and laughs, but says nothing. The Musicians, prompted by the Singer's questions, speak for her. So her conflicting feelings, detached from her person, are given economically at one remove.

35 *I always withdraw* — the Corporal puns on Grusha's words. The withdrawal he means is coitus interruptus. His speeches are sexually suggestive and full of menace.

36 *In this house I decide* — by making the wife act normally while the audience is aware of the approaching danger, Brecht builds up suspense.

38 *a thousand piastres* — the reward offered by Prince Kazbeki for the capture of the Governor's son.

39 *Grusha Vachnadze decided to be the child's mother* — it is only here, when she is forced to do so by the Ironshirts, that Grusha decides to accept full responsibility for Michael.

39 *Nobody wants to take you* — as when Grusha made her pledge to Simon, Brecht puts a plain, eloquent poem into her mouth at this moment of decision. This is a moving scene as she takes off the baby's fine clothes, wraps him in rags and christens him into the fraternity of poverty with icy water.

40 *One rope is broken* — Brecht constructed a real, practicable bridge for this scene in his own production, though it might seem to invite mime, or some other non-representational, alienated device. The practicable bridge was in his case stylistically in keeping with the rest of the staging.

41 *Shouts from a distance* — with the Ironshirts audibly on her

heels Grusha has no time to think of the risks of crossing the
dangerous bridge. This is the climax of the chase.

41 *If the gulf is deep* — the Song of the Rotten Bridge is a verse
soliloquy, making it clear that Grusha is wholly committed to a
future together with the child but uncertain about how they will
survive.

42 *Your father's a thief* — Grusha sings this song as a lullaby.
Its burden is reconciliation and universal peace, with an end to
violence (tiger/foal, snake/mother) and social differences (thief,
whore/nice people).

Scene 4

43 *she thought to herself* — the Singer, as omniscient narrator,
sketches the welcome Grusha expects in a hypothetical
conversation as she heads for her brother's house.

43 *sat down to a meal* — there is a striking visual contrast between
the plump couple and the haggard, exhausted Grusha. This was,
according to Angelika Hurwicz who was Brecht's Grusha at the
Berliner Ensemble, the only point at which the word alientation
was used during the entire rehearsals. Brecht felt that in the first
rehearsals Grusha's brother and his wife seemed too emotional, too
worked-up at the state of the Grusha when she arrived, so he used
his alienating rehearsal technique of having the two prefix their
lines with 'the man said' and 'the woman said' to tone down their
response to something like stunned surprise at the unexpected
arrival.

44 *Has it got a father?* — Grusha shakes her head, meaning that
the Governor is dead. Her brother assumes however that Michael is
her illegitimate son and begins to think of a cover story for his
pious wife.

44 *As long as it's not scarlet fever* — the Sister-in-Law's piety is
coupled with utter selfishness. Her prolonged, hostile interrogation
ignores Grusha's state of collapse. The scene, with her harping on
contagious diseases, finds a line between pathos and black farce.

45 *She has a good heart* — we only have the Brother's word for
this since his wife never displays kindness.

45 *The winter was long/The winter was short* — long because of
the cold and discomfort, short because she would be without a
roof over her head as soon as it ended.

46 *Stay wisely in between* — Grusha's weaving song contains a
strategy for survival: keep in the middle of the pack and make

yourself inconspicuous. It is a reminder of Grusha's concern for Simon, and it clarifies her need to adopt a 'low profile' in her brother's house, where even feeling cold will be taken as an offence.

46 *till the snow melts* — the spring thaw will turn Grusha out of the house. When the appropriate sound effect is heard, the audience knows what it means.

47 *mention the Ironshirt* — the Brother has not told his wife that Grusha is wanted for having laid out the Ironshirt to save Michael.

48 *A rubber stamp makes all the difference* — this is anachronistic, perhaps an ironic dig at German officialdom's obsession with rubber stamps, without which even the most trivial document is invalid. Once Grusha has a marriage certificate the neighbours will no longer talk and Michael will no longer be conspicuous.

48 *as a pear tree comes by the sparrows* — having agreed to the sham marriage, Grusha ruefully reflects that it was not in the first instance inclination, but the Puritan principle 'Waste not, want not' that led to her having Michael on her hands. The effect on her own life is now being brought home to her.

48 *A space divided by a partition* — the stage is split into two halves (see illustration). Thus the supposedly comatose husband can react to the wedding reception next door, and the audience sees all. A situation rich in comic possibilities.

49 *drying her tears* — the Mother-in-Law's respectability like the Sister-in-Law's piety, is bogus, in this case a mere pretext for extorting another 200 piastres. Brecht wants to show a mercenary, capitalist society.

50 *in Latin* — the trappings throughout are those of the Catholic Church.

50 *Extreme Unction* — in the Catholic Church the sacrament administered to the dying. The coming monk is keen to move from the marriage ceremony stratight into the administration of Extreme Unction.

51 *he was lying there like a corpse* — the danger that the passing riders might be recruiters induced the feigned coma.

52 *he charges a fortune* — the bourgeois professions, here the ministry, and later in the play medicine, are wholly mercenary. The services of religion are traded as a saleable commodity in Grusinia.

53 *but against disorder* — though they are historic foes, their common class interest decrees that they close ranks when revolution threatens their status. Class consciousness outweighs patriotism.

53 *we'll have to pay for the war* — that wars are always fought at the people's expense is a theme that runs through Brecht's mature plays.

55 *It's against nature* — this indicates that the marriage has not been consummated.

56 *almanac* — a handbook of conventional wisdom, covering all aspects of peasant life in Germany, or in this case Grusinia.

56 *As the months passed by, the child grew up* — this poem in free rhythms evokes the passage of time and the fading of Simon's memory. It is his face Grusha sees in the water.

56 *Heads-off* — the game re-enacts the death of Michael's father. Michael wants a turn at beheading, but it must be done with a light touch so that Grusha's laughter makes sense, the laughter in turn is needed to make Simon's entrance effective.

57 *They found better fish than me* — Simon still inclines to speak in proverbs, or at least images. The conversation avoids the direct modes of address, I or you, and this keeps the emotional key low. Grusha's obliqueness, though its meaning is clear to the audience, leaves Simon in the dark, and he refuses to cross the river to meet her.

59 *it blows through every crack* — sexual innuendo. Simon believes the child is Grusha's.

59 *Hear what she thought and did not say* — the Singer reverts to his earlier function, telling what Grusha might have said to Simon.

60 *Who will try the case?* — the Singer ends with a 'trailer' for the next scene.

Scene 5

61 *Easter Sunday of the great revolt* — the classic Hollywood sub-title here would be 'Meanwhile, on the outskirts of the capital . . .', for the play shifts back in time to scene 2 and tells the contemporaneous story of Azdak the judge. This time shift shows Brecht's disregard for Aristotelian structure and for the unities of time and place. Arkady Cheidze has, of course, said (p.8) he is going to tell two stories, but the two elements could have been interwoven. Instead Brecht stresses the individual stories (epics) by allotting each its own stage time. This is the only play in which he does this.

61 *village clerk* — in these ancient times an educated man, and in Marxist categories a member of the intelligentsia. Drunk and in rags, Azdak is established right away as an eccentric, rebellious figure. In the Berliner Ensemble production Ernst Busch played both the Singer and Azdak. This has since become standard practice. Brecht's only comment is that Azdak must be played by the best *actor*, not the best singer.

61 *would go through the walls* — the stage directions show the Fugitive as a comic caricature of the helpless aristocrat, reduced by fear to a slobbering jelly in which it is impossible to recognise the Grand Murderer or Grand Thief of Azdak's later self-accusation (p.64).

61 *Grand Duke* — dramatic irony since, unbeknown to Adzak, it *is* the Grand Duke.

62 *a decent human being* — in the simplified social structure of the play white hands indicate a landowner, and for Azdak the only decent people are the workers, with whom he classes himself. Grusha was given away by her hands when she pretended to be an aristocrat in scene 3 (p.30).

62 *Am hunted* — Brecht's German distinguishes the ruling classes by their clipped speech and short, incomplete sentences. The translation follows this. (See note on language in the commentary.)

62 *Leech makes a proposition* — the poor man scratches his leech-bites till his fingers bleed, and the rich man (leech) has the gall to make him a proposition.

62 *Especially what they call weeds* — the curious logic of exterminating rabbits because they eat weeds, sets the comic note for Azdak's witty dumbfounding of the slow-witted Shauva.

62 *I'm a man of intellect* — Azdak is offended by the suggestion that he has a good heart, which he implies is incompatible with being an intellectual. There was a touch of this in Brecht himself. Azdak's later actions must be taken to emanate from the intellect rather than the heart — in contrast to Grusha's throughout the play.

63 *how a poor man behaves?* — Azdak proceeds to show how a poor man's table manners are conditioned by his social situation, and, incidentally, demonstrates what Brecht means by 'gestus', namely the essential elements in a character's behaviour which the actor has to identify and reproduce if he is to get the social implications of his role across. The Fugitive gets a lesson in Brechtian acting.

64 *like Pontius Pilate into the Creed* — unintentionally and undeservedly. The Turk's belonging to the right class is fortuitously cancelled out by being a foreigner, another comment on the erratic nature of class justice.

64 *A new age has come* — Azdak has discovered that he has harboured the Grand Duke. He decides to make a clean breast of it because he imagines that the revolution has taken place and will bring about absolute justice, managed by the people without any police force. People he meets think his utopian pronouncements are ridiculous and possibly mad.

65 *Here's the judge* — this is Judge Orbeliani whose fate is mentioned in passing by the Adjutant on page 21.

65 *stop 'bothering' us* — Azdak fails to recognise this warning.

66 *Too long a war! And no justice!* — these are the two reasons Azdak gives for the Persian revolution. They apply equally to the October Revolution of 1917 in Russia, and they introduce the theme of disorder and justice which is central to the story of the judge.

66 *but the helmets have been paid for* — the first stanza of the Persian song asks why the sons do not bleed nor the daughters weep any more, and the implied answer is that the Grand King's war of expansion has bled the populace dry while the rulers prospered. The helmets have been paid for by heavy taxes which have ended up in the pockets of profiteers. The second stanza tells of peace which brings no respite to the people. Incompetents rule in luxury, while the economy flounders. The song is a revolutionary indictment of the feudal system in both war and peace.

67 *our carpet weavers caught the 'Persian disease'* — the carpet weavers' rising was put down by the Ironshirts, so the proleterian revolution has failed. The beating 'to pulp for two piastres per weaver' echoes Great War atrocities when Austrian soldiers hanged Serbian dissidents for a few cigarettes a head. Azdak now grasps the situation.

68 *I let him escape?* — Azdak changes his tune, reminding the soldiers that he let the Grand Duke get away. He is no hero, and he is more concerned with survival than principles.

68 *burst out laughing* — the Ironshirts are mercenaries, unpredictable, committed to their own interests rather than to any cause. They are content with a sadistic joke without actually harming Azdak physically. In rehearsal Brecht was asked why they don't kill him. There are various reasons, he replied, and the first is that it would mean the end of the play. But if you are that way inclined there are psychological reasons, for example they are tired of killing, they are drunk, they get a kick out of the power of life and death. And Azdak impresses them . . .

68 *Permit me a serious word* — the Fat Prince gives an account of recent events as seen by the clique that has come to power in the coup.

69 *They've got the jitters* — because Fat Prince feels insecure with the Grand Duke still at large he is willing to let the Ironshirts, who stand here for the people, elect the new judge. Since Azdak, albeit inadvertently, put the Ironshirts in this position of unwonted influence, they let him join in the fun. Azdak's confidence grows as he grasps what is going on. He too is a joker.

69 *the Judge being appointed* — Azdak indulges his beguiling gift of the gab. He seems to be saying that the law is an inane formality, and can only survive if its outward form is respected. To use a real criminal for a mock trial would amount to disrespect to the law. Azdak manages to argue for form without acknowledging content, but it is a comic passage setting up the mock trial, so it should not be read too literally.

70 *unmistakable gait of the Grand Duke* — the role Azdak is going to play is first introduced visually. He later mimics his speech mannerisms.

70 *From the point of view of taste, I mean* — Azdak as the Grand Duke has opened the proceedings in a tone of farce. The Nephew is not sure that this is in good taste. They are, after all, trying one of his peers.

71 *Only at my command* — Azdak is being ironic here, making it clear that the Grand Duke is only nominally in command, and spreading the blame to his lieutenants. It amuses the Ironshirts.

71 *Only telling the truth!* — the irony of the situation is that Azdak makes the Grand Duke defend himself in terms a proletarian revolutionary might have chosen to attack the system, and is even getting the Ironshirts on his side, as they recognise the truth in his picture of corruption and profiteering.

72 *Sentence passed. No appeal* — having conducted his prosecution in rounded sentences to ingratiate himself with the Ironshirts, the Nephew loses his composure and reverts to the natural clipped tones of the ruling class, as Azdak sarcastically notes.

72 *howl like wolf* — the judge is a watchdog, the exploitative ruling classes the wolves.

72 *War lost only for Grusinia* — this is a constant theme in Brecht's mature plays. In war, the people always lose.

72 *The wicker from a bottle on his head* — again Brecht makes a visual point. The wicker hat makes a clown of the judge, keeping the element of farce to the fore. The Ironshirts motives here need not be too closely questioned. They have been allowed to choose the Judge and they know it cannot last. Azdak's performance with its home truths amused them, so they give him his chance.

73 *Great houses turn to ashes* — the song underlines the context, two years of civil war and social upheaval, in which Azdak will pronounce justice.

73 *peeling an apple* — Brecht establishes the situation visually.
Azdak disregards formality and eats an apple in the Judge's seat,
which prepares the audience for his unconventional procedure.

73 *I receive* — Azdak adopts the traditional Grusinian practice
of accepting bribes — without, it transpires, guaranteeing results.

73 *an inexcusable professional mistake* — medicine has been
shown to be a business, so the unprofessional conduct was failing
to charge, beside which operating on the wrong leg is insignificant.
The blackmailer's skill in extorting money suggests, Azdak notes,
an aptitude for medicine. The scene is written as ironic farce, and
all concerned get their deserts in commonsense terms.

75 *Beware of willing judges* — the song covers Azdak's journey
from one hearing to the next. Its burden is that only a disinterested
outsider can extract justice from the corrupt system.

75 *Justice* — traditionally represented as veiled and blindfolded
woman.

76 *I said I liked the little roan* — the Innkeeper steadfastly refuses
to take Azdak's persistent hints. This is the same man as was seen
charging exorbitant prices in scene 3 (p.29).

76 *deliberate assault with a dangerous weapon* — the flourish with
which Azdak pronounces the waggle of Ludovica's bottom to be
criminal looks dangerously like male chauvinism, but Brecht sees
her provocative appearance as a result of a life of bourgeois
indolence and luxury. Her evidence sounds like a fabrication too.

77 *No more did the Lower Orders* — the excellent but free
translation of the song loses the much quoted phrase 'the good
bad judge Azdak' at the end of the second stanza. The first two
stanzas praise Azdak's Robin Hood style of justice, the third points
forward to Robber Irakli's axe in the next episode. Sometimes
advocacy fails and only violence can achieve (social) justice.

79 *strikes straight at the Court's heart* — the ham for the old
woman is really a matter of redistribution of wealth, and in
sanctioning the 'miracle' in his last hearing Azdak pronounces his
most socialist verdict. Here again the trappings are farcical, like
the unchallenged presence of the robber in court.

80 *Well, well, well, did Azdak/Measure with false scales* — the
Singer and Musicians drive home the message; Azdak, sitting
under the gallows as a constant reminder of the fate of his
predecessor, for two years weighs in false scales to counterbalance
the bias of the legal system in favour of the rich.

80 *Court of Justice* — Azdak's judical progress through Grusinia
has brought him back to the capital, Nukha.

80 *your days of slavery* — the days of Azdak's justice are
paradoxically the days of Shauva's slavery because, Azdak explains,
Shauva is by nature a bootlicker and a law-and-order man. This is
rather unfair to poor, mild Shauva.

81 *The Song of Chaos* — the narrator of the ballad is a nobleman,
hence his appeal to the General to restore order. The song, which
may be based on an ancient Egyptian original, is a catalogue of
revolutionary social change. Azdak observes that Grusinia's chance
to reorganise society has passed.

81 *The son of the nobleman* — a reminder of Michael and Grusha.

82 *An army to restore order* — this Persian alliance was previously
reported at Grusha's wedding (p.53).

82 *the have-nots to get away with everything* — Azdak assesses
his own role as having been champion of the poor against the rich.

82 *The fear of death is upon me* — just as in the episode of the
gibbet (p.67), Azdak thinks first of saving his skin and is
immediately (perhaps ironically) servile to Natella Abashvili.

Scene 6

84 *doesn't understand anything* — Grusha is offhand, whereas
Simon is conciliatory throughout this exchange.

85 *a packet of money* — the Corporal almost had the reward
offered by Prince Kazbeki in his hands when Grusha knocked him
out in scene 3. Now he could make money by identifying Grusha,
but if he did he would incriminate himself as one of the ursurper
Kazbeki's former henchmen.

86 *lowest ever seen in the judge's robe* — the Cook and Grusha
are hoping for Azdak with whom Grusha has a chance, but the
Lawyers are hoping the restored Grand Duke will appoint a
proper judge. From here Brecht keeps the outcome in the balance
to the end.

86 *three farmers bring up the rear* — these are the farmers he
fined in the previous scene (p.79).

86 *at each other's throats, dogs?* — Azdak now has nothing to
lose, so he turns sarcastic and defiant.

87 *A certain Azdak in Nukha* — Brecht had used a despatch rider
as *deus ex machina* once before, in *The Threepenny Opera*. By a
miraculous coincidence the Grand Duke now appoints Azdak
Judge as a reward for saving his life in scene 5. The tables are
turned and the farmers, who know power when they see it, are
led off, bowing humbly.

88 *If I know you are good* — Azdak has extorted two bribes, He now elicits the Lawyer's fee and remarks, ambiguously, that it will affect the hearing. The audience are thus reminded that Grusha is up against big money.

88 *Nature herself* — the Lawyer has prepared a high-flown speech in praise of the ties of blood, which Azdak curtly interrupts.

89 *Work as well as he could* — Grusha can only counter the Lawyer's eloquence with an artless account of the simple upbringing she has given Michael.

89 *the sleepless nights* — the Governor's Wife thinks only of her own emotions which are pretended rather than real.

89 *It's proof of human feeling* — Azdak's comment is ironic, but the Lawyer takes it at face value.

90 *the result of whoring?* — all Grusha's answers are frank, but even if she were capable of duplicity there would be no answer to this question.

91 *a funeral supper* — a free meal. Azdak bends the laws to provide justice for the poor, but this does not prevent him from wishing they could pay.

91 *Czarevitch* — the eldest son of the Czar.

91 *But 'a fart has no nose'* — the corrupt cannot smell their own corruption. Simon has expressed himself in pithy sayings from the start, and Azdak accepts his challenge to a contest in proverbs, some of them invented. By comparing Azdak to the horsefly, the angler, the Czar and the nose, Simon accuses him of selfishness and profiteering. Azdak's proverbs suggest that the most you can do is make the best of a bad job. Heroics are out. Simon has the last word, but Azdak fines him for it.

92 *don't know any more about justice than I do, that's clear* — Azdak is touched by the truth of Grusha's accusation, just as he is touched earlier by the truth of the Old Woman's calling her ham a miracle, and a rapport is established between them.

92 *You bribe-taker!* — the irony here is that Grusha, with her first flood of eloquence in the play, expresses sentiments that are close to Azdak's own. He has called the Farmers and Ironshirts dogs and bootlickers (p.86), he has called Shauva a weak lackey (p.80), and his Persian Song and Song of Chaos painted exactly the same picture of social injustice. This is why he beams and ends up beating time to Grusha's diatribe. This takes the element of fear out of the situation, but not the suspense, since it is not clear how he proposes to bring about a suitable solution.

94 *But not the light* — Grusha's thoughts are given indirectly here,

as they were when she left Michael on the peasants' doorstep
(p.34). The Singer can formulate what she feels more tellingly.
Azdak then responds as if he had worked out from her silence
what she is thinking. It is a dialogue full of artifice.

95 *Am I to tear him to pieces?* — finally it is Grusha's concern
for the child's well-being that gives Azdak his cue to find in her
favour. The audience is with him.

95 *The Garden of Azdak* — so instead of the 'miserable slum
houses' being replaced by a palace garden (p.11), the Abashvili
estate will become a children's playground.

96 *Have I divorced the wrong ones?* — Azdak's mock surprise
is in tune with the combination of farce and fairy tale.

97 *the meaning of the ancient song* — Brecht brings the first
and last scenes together, suggesting that the award of the child
to the mother who has fostered him is analogous to the award
of the valley to the fruit growers, which is now assumed to be
the outcome of 'The Struggle for the Valley'. Both are
rational decisions.

Illustrations

The photographs on the following pages (by Percy Paukschta) are of the Berliner Ensemble production directed by Brecht and designed by Karl von Appen.

1. Scene 1 (p.3): The kolchos peasants debate the future of the valley. On the right the goat-breeders with their cheese, on the left the fruit-growers whose agronomist with her rolled up plans is near the centre, behind her a Red Army soldier.

2. Scene 2 (p.12): Simon Chachava accosts Grusha at the city gate as she brings home the goose. Though there was no attempt at illusionistic realism, the parts which stood for the whole — here the facade for the church (on the left) and the gate for the city — were finished in carefully researched detail. The stylised architectural wedge on the backcloth represents Nukha as a towering beehive of a city.

3. Scene 3 (p.26): Grusha continues on her way with the child on her back. A backcloth of mountains and pines in the style of Chinese ink-drawings indicates the northern mountains. As Grusha walked on the revolving stage the peasant's cottage travelled towards her from behind the backcloth.

4. Scene 3 (p.27): The cottage has stopped at the right of the stage and Grusha has put down the baby and her bundle and is haggling over milk with the peasant.

5. Scene 3 (p.34): The peasant woman has taken the baby in her arms, but her husband turns his back on her as she decides to keep it. Grusha observes from behind a convenient tree-stump. The landscape on the backcloth has changed to mark her progress.

6. Scene 4 (p.44): Grusha, supported by a stableman, enters her brother's cottage. This time the interior of the hut is shown, with a dish on the table and a napkin round Lavrenti's neck. The grouping

clearly shows the concern of the stableman and the coolness of the fat couple, especially the Sister-in-Law who keeps her hands resolutely clasped.

7. Scene 4 (p.51): The wedding. Yussup lies screened by a curtain in bed. Grusha and the Mother-in-Law pick up the cakes while Michael cowers in the background. The tub for the back-scrubbing scene is in the background. The wedding guests are huddled round the monk in the next room. Brecht found that keeping the guests confined in a small space on the otherwise open stage brought out the grotesque, farcical tone of the scene.

8. Scene 4 (p.58): The returning Simon Chachava and Grusha face one another across the river which is indicated by rows of reeds. The beautifully managed separation in this potentially emotional scene helps to keep it cool.

9. Scene 5 (p.75): The Innkeeper hands Azdak money as he sits in the Judge's seat. Ludovika is at the centre of the stage and the accused Stableman at the right.

10. Scene 5 (p.79): Azdak sits in the Judge's seat under the gallows, to the left of him the Bandit Irakli with his axe, to the right, crouching, the Old Woman.

11. Scene 6 (p.95): The chalk circle test. The child looks at Grusha, the Lawyers and the Cook and Simon are poised, urging on their candidates while the old couple, back to back, look on casually. The backcloth makes it clear that the action is back in Nukha, and the rough wooden gate at the left indicates that the pomp of the second scene has been ravaged by the civil wars.

1

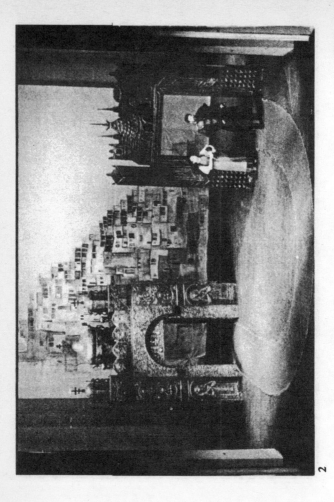

2

6

3

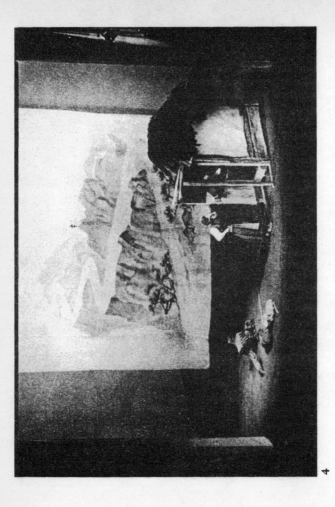

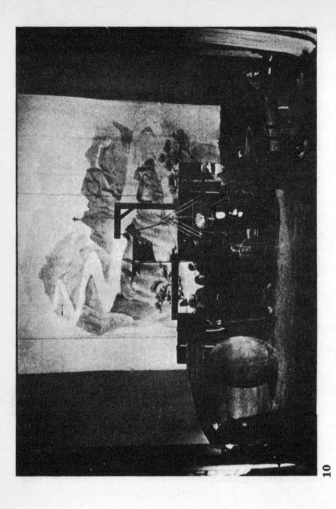

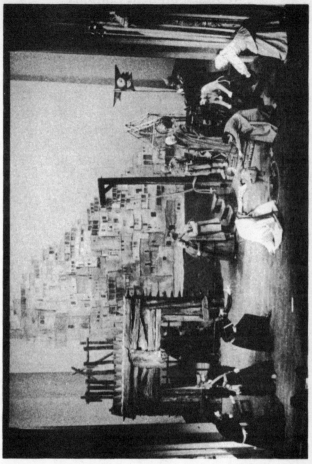

11

Methuen Student Editions

Methuen Modern Plays
include work by

Jean Anouilh
John Arden
Margaretta D'Arcy
Peter Barnes
Sebastian Barry
Dermot Bolger
Brendan Behan
Edward Bond
Bertolt Brecht
Howard Brenton
Anthony Burgess
Simon Burke
Jim Cartwright
Caryl Churchill
Noël Coward
Lucinda Coxon
Sarah Daniels
Nick Darke
Nick Dear
Shelagh Delaney
David Edgar
David Eldridge
Dario Fo
Michael Frayn
John Godber
Paul Godfrey
David Greig
John Guare
Peter Handke
David Harrower
Jonathan Harvey
Iain Heggie
Declan Hughes
Terry Johnson
Sarah Kane
Charlotte Keatley
Barrie Keeffe
Howard Korder

Robert Lepage
Stephen Lowe
Doug Lucie
Martin McDonagh
John McGrath
Terrence McNally
David Mamet
Patrick Marber
Arthur Miller
Mtwa, Ngema & Simon
Tom Murphy
Phyllis Nagy
Peter Nichols
Joseph O'Connor
Joe Orton
Louise Page
Joe Penhall
Luigi Pirandello
Stephen Poliakoff
Franca Rame
Mark Ravenhill
Philip Ridley
Reginald Rose
David Rudkin
Willy Russell
Jean-Paul Sartre
Sam Shepard
Wole Soyinka
Shelagh Stephenson
C. P. Taylor
Theatre de Complicite
Theatre Workshop
Sue Townsend
Judy Upton
Timberlake Wertenbaker
Roy Williams
Victoria Wood

Methuen World Classics
include

Jean Anouilh (two volumes)
John Arden (two volumes)
Arden & D'Arcy
Brendan Behan
Aphra Behn
Bertolt Brecht (seven volumes)
Büchner
Bulgakov
Calderón
Čapek
Anton Chekhov
Noël Coward (eight volumes)
Eduardo De Filippo
Max Frisch
John Galsworthy
Gogol
Gorky
Harley Granville Barker
  (two volumes)
Henrik Ibsen (six volumes)
Lorca (three volumes)

Marivaux
Mustapha Matura
David Mercer (two volumes)
Arthur Miller (five volumes)
Molière
Musset
Peter Nichols (two volumes)
Clifford Odets
Joe Orton
A. W. Pinero
Luigi Pirandello
Terence Rattigan
  (two volumes)
W. Somerset Maugham
  (two volumes)
August Strindberg
  (three volumes)
J. M. Synge
Ramón del Valle-Inclán
Frank Wedekind
Oscar Wilde

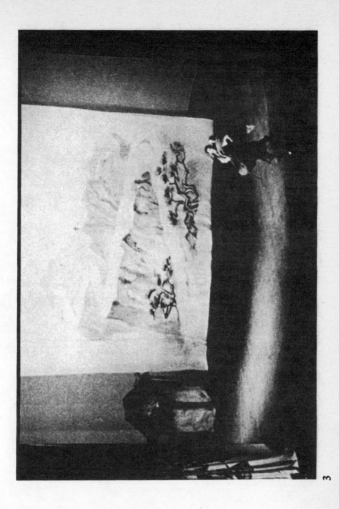

3

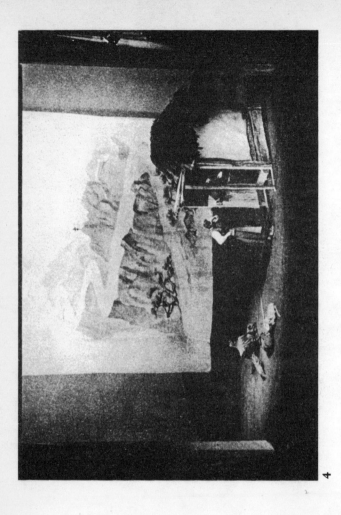

4

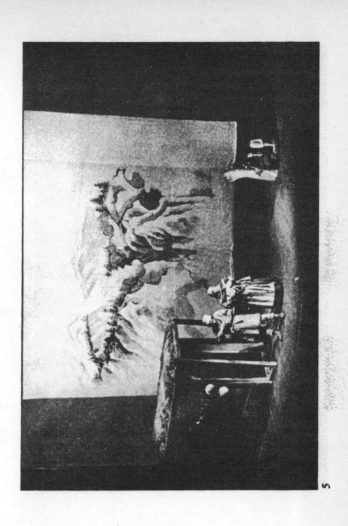

5

6

6

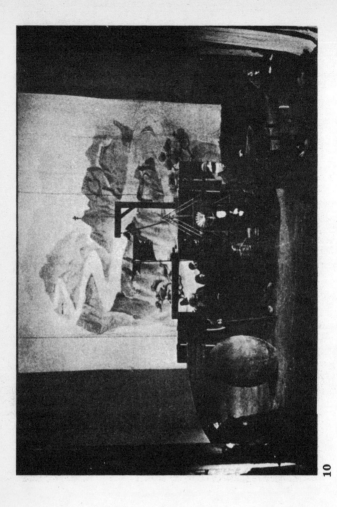

11

Methuen Student Editions

Jean Aniuilh	*Antigone*
John Arden	*Serjeant Musgrave's Dance*
Alan Ayckbourn	*Confusions*
Aphra Behn	*The Rover*
Edward Bond	*Lear*
Bertolt Brecht	*The Caucasian Chalk Circle*
	Life of Galileo
	Mother Courage and her Children
Anton Chekhov	*The Cherry Orchard*
Caryl Churchill	*Top Girls*
Shelagh Delaney	*A Taste of Honey*
John Galsworthy	*Strife*
Robert Holman	*Across Oka*
Henrik Ibsen	*A Doll's House*
Charlotte Keatley	*My Mother Said I Never Should*
Bernard Kops	*Dreams of Anne Frank*
Federico García Lorca	*Blood Wedding*
	The House of Bernarda Alba
	(bilingual edition)
John Marston	*The Malcontent*
Willy Russell	*Blood Brothers*
Wole Soyinka	*Death and the King's Horseman*
August Strindberg	*The Father*
J. M. Synge	*The Playboy of the Western World*
Oscar Wilde	*The Importance of Being Earnest*
Tennessee Williams	*A Streetcar Named Desire*
	The Glass Menagerie
Timberlake Wertenbaker	*Our Country's Good*

Methuen Modern Plays
include work by

Methuen World Classics
include

Jean Anouilh (two volumes)
John Arden (two volumes)
Arden & D'Arcy
Brendan Behan
Aphra Behn
Bertolt Brecht (seven volumes)
Büchner
Bulgakov
Calderón
Čapek
Anton Chekhov
Noël Coward (eight volumes)
Eduardo De Filippo
Max Frisch
John Galsworthy
Gogol
Gorky
Harley Granville Barker
  (two volumes)
Henrik Ibsen (six volumes)
Lorca (three volumes)

Marivaux
Mustapha Matura
David Mercer (two volumes)
Arthur Miller (five volumes)
Molière
Musset
Peter Nichols (two volumes)
Clifford Odets
Joe Orton
A. W. Pinero
Luigi Pirandello
Terence Rattigan
  (two volumes)
W. Somerset Maugham
  (two volumes)
August Strindberg
  (three volumes)
J. M. Synge
Ramón del Valle-Inclán
Frank Wedekind
Oscar Wilde